CREATING AUTHENTIC RELATIONSHIPS WITH PARENTS OF YOUNG CHILDREN

Dealing with parents can be scary and intimidating, especially when you are relatively new to your role, but it can also be hugely rewarding. What do you need to know? Which barriers are you likely to face? Most importantly, how can you nurture a positive and authentic relationship with parents and carers where you genuinely work together for the best interests of the child?

Written by authors who have experienced being on both sides of the fence, as educators and as parents, this practical book takes a frank approach to recognising the turbulent world of parenting and shines a light on issues that are, all too often, dismissed. It considers the pragmatic, kind, and caring ways that educational settings can support parents' struggles, as well as benefitting from their wide-ranging knowledge and capabilities. With activities and reflections included throughout, the book invites the reader to consider their practice, and to look at their relationships with parents with fresh eyes, all whilst keeping the child in mind.

With a focus on celebrating the value of truly listening and forming authentic relationships, this book will be essential reading for early years' educators, childminders, primary teachers, TAs, and SENCOs.

Carla Solvason is Senior Lecturer in the Centre for Children and Families at the University of Worcester, UK.

Johanna Cliffe is Lecturer at The Learning Institute, a partner organisation of the University of Worcester, UK.

T0383535

CREATING AUTHENTIC RELATIONSHIPS WITH PARENTS OF YOUNG CHILDREN

A PRACTICAL GUIDE FOR EDUCATORS

Carla Solvason and Johanna Cliffe

Routledge
Taylor & Francis Group

LONDON AND NEW YORK

Cover image: SARAH HOYLE

First published 2023
by Routledge
4 Park Square, Milton Park, Abingdon, Oxon OX14 4RN

and by Routledge
605 Third Avenue, New York, NY 10158

Routledge is an imprint of the Taylor & Francis Group, an informa business

British Library Cataloguing-in-Publication Data
A catalogue record for this book is available from the British Library

Library of Congress Cataloging-in-Publication Data
Names: Solvason, Carla, author. | Cliffe, Johanna, 1978- author.
Title: Creating authentic relationships with parents of young children:
a practical guide for educators/Carla Solvason and Johanna Cliffe.
Description: Abingdon, Oxon; New York, NY: Routledge, 2023. |
Includes bibliographical references and index. |
Identifiers: LCCN 2022013031 (print) | LCCN 2022013032 (ebook) |
ISBN 9781032042688 (hardback) | ISBN 9781032042626 (paperback) |
ISBN 9781003191209 (ebook)
Subjects: LCSH: Parent-teacher relationships. | Early childhood
education–Study and teaching. | Home and school.
Classification: LCC LC226 .S65 2023 (print) | LCC LC226 (ebook) |
DDC 371.19/2–dc23/eng/20220624
LC record available at https://lccn.loc.gov/2022013031
LC ebook record available at https://lccn.loc.gov/2022013032

ISBN: 978-1-032-04268-8 (hbk)
ISBN: 978-1-032-04262-6 (pbk)
ISBN: 978-1-003-19120-9 (ebk)

DOI: 10.4324/9781003191209

Typeset in Palatina and Scala Sans
by Deanta Global Publishing Services, Chennai, India

With special thanks to Emma Laurence who began this quest with us and to our children, who got stuck with not-so-perfect parents

Contents

Welcome to Our Book

Carla Solvason

This is a book written by two mothers. It is important to state that first, so you understand that what follows isn't just a pile of theoretical claptrap, but a book based upon (sometimes painful) lived experience. As well as being parents, Johanna and I are also teachers, researchers, and academics; and as such we aim to provide you with a multi-faceted view of parent partnership in educational settings. We unashamedly have a key aim with this book, which is to highlight the importance of recognising emotion and valuing kindness and care within the relationships that you, as educators, form with parents. It is also intended to make you more aware of the prescriptive view of 'the parent' that has emerged through a myopic focus upon academic results, and to celebrate the value of truly listening to those people who know the child best.

Throughout this book we chiefly use the term *practitioner* rather than teacher, this is so as not to exclude anyone involved in the laudable task of caring for and educating children. This book is relevant to you whether you are a teaching assistant, nursery nurse, manager, room lead, year group lead, teacher, or head teacher. (And I've no doubt there are many other titles I could have added to that list – sorry if I missed out yours.) Basically, anyone reading this book, if you have ever spoken to a parent or written a message for a parent of a child in your care – yes, this book applies to you. Likewise, this book is not context-specific, but could apply to those working in a secondary school just as readily as it does those in a primary school, or a children's club, or a nursery. It is good to remember that parents don't suddenly switch their feelings off when a child turns 11. Therefore, we refer to 'settings' throughout, again, as an all-encompassing term. We are confident that this little book (with big ideas) will provide food for thought for practitioners working with children of all ages.

As parents who, although fully qualified for the role *on paper*, regularly failed to fit the mould of 'the good parent' that most settings prescribe, we bring the often-challenging task of parenting under the spotlight; and in doing so task practitioners with questioning their assumptions about what parents need and how they believe they should behave. We draw upon our personal experience as well as our own previous research (which presents the voices of those currently working in early years, primary, and specialist school settings), to add validity and depth to the issues under investigation. We encourage you, often, to reflect upon your own values and your own experiences. We also urge you to take your thinking forward in some practical ways, through directed activities. It would be even better if those activities can involve your wider setting and its colleagues and impact, in any small way, upon the culture. We've lots to work on, but first, please let me share with you my own experience of being a not-so-perfect mother.

REMEMBER, BEING A PARENT IS NO WALK IN THE PARK

We all know those Earth Mother types, all smiles, swanning about in their flouncy skirts with babies virtually dropping out of their pockets. Their brood of children is a little dishevelled in a rough-and-tumble sort of way, but happy; whilst Earth Mother finds time to bake vegan scones for the school fete, knit all her children's clothes, and attend yoga four times a week. And she usually heads up the Parent Teacher Association, or whatever it has been rebranded as these days. She makes motherhood look a pure joy and totally effortless. The truth is that for most parents, rearing children is quite the opposite of effortless. Even Earth Mother will have her bad days, she's just better at hiding it than those of us that have it written all over our faces. On a sliding scale, parenthood is somewhere between 'okay, manageable, I've got this sussed now' and 'I give up, I cannot do this one more day' at any given moment. Now that is not to negate those moments of pure, heart-bursting delight, that make it all worthwhile, but many who are quick to judge can forget just how hard being a parent is. It can be totally exhausting ... you never get to clock off.

My sons are now (legally, at least) adults. They are reasonably intact, but I often feel that they survived despite my parenting, rather than thrived because of it. For much of their school lives I was a single parent, frequently mired in difficult relationships and even more difficult break-ups (yes, I had poor attachment as a child, but we would need to add a couple more volumes of this book if I were to go into detail about that here). My nearest relatives were 200 miles away, so there was no support there. I was on my own. Although my children would see their father regularly, I had full financial responsibility for them and I worked full-time, as a teacher. For a while this meant that my typical day entailed getting the boys up and ready to leave the house at 6.30am, driving across the city to drop them at their dad's (who would walk them to their school), before driving back across the city to teach all day (at a school where there were many, *many* challenging children). At the end of the day I would then drive back across the city to pick up the boys from their after-school club at around 6pm, drive them back home, feed them, bathe them, and get them to bed with a quick story (which *I* read them or told them ... if you've ever tried struggling over a school reading book with a child when you are both tired and narky you will totally understand why). There were no impromptu phonics sessions, no adorable bake-offs, no tripping through the park to collect autumnal leaves; well, not on a weekday, anyway. I had nothing left to give at the end of a very long day.

So why am I telling you this? I am sharing this situation because during this time as a 'broken and in the process of negotiating a new life' family, whenever my boys produced a note from school expecting me to knock up a quick '19th century school child' outfit for the next day, or when I had to magic up pizza cooking ingredients, or do some research on tawny owls ('which had to be done by *tomorrow* or their teacher would tell them off' – best read in a whiny voice), it immediately sent me into the 'I give up' zone. I was barely coping; any extra demand was likely to tip me over the edge. Every time I received a caustic comment in my children's reading books berating me for not listening to them read more often (that happened *a lot*), I wanted to tell that teacher exactly what they could do with that reading record. I vividly remember a parents' evening during this difficult time where the teacher's opening comment was "well his handwriting is scruffy" as she then proceeded to annihilate most aspects of my son's personality. He was a six-year-old whose life was in freefall. He desperately needed kindness, support, and security within his school life and instead all we received, as a struggling and broken family, were stark demands and bucket loads of criticism. And I, on the surface, a well-educated teacher who should *know better*. I should have been one of the 'good parents' who behaved in the expected manner.

In my own experience, in my conversations with other parents and in the assignments that I read by students preparing to be educators, the language used to describe the parent–teacher relationship is frequently judgemental and confrontational. Somewhere in the battle for good grades, excellent Ofsted reports and the 'typically' developing child, parents and teachers have lost sight of the fact that they are both meant to be fighting on the same side. We have lost our vision of the moral duty of care that those in education take on. This could well be (as Stephen Ball, 2006, commented wryly), because *values* have now been replaced by *value*, "except for when values can be seen to add value". Both parties, ultimately, want what is best for the child, so why can it so often feel that they are pulling in totally different directions?

REFLECTION POINT

Let's pause for a second and consider the concept of 'parent partnership'. What does this term mean to you? What does it mean to your setting? In your view, at this point, what does parent partnership 'look like' in practice?

WHY PARENT PARTNERSHIP?

The importance of 'parent partnership' is seldom disputed; in fact, at one point it became so embedded within the standard educational vernacular that some began to wonder whether teachers had decided that they just couldn't face the job on their own anymore. For all parents, maintaining involvement in their children's education and care is crucial, therefore partnership working is an imperative in education. However, my idea of what parent partnership should *look like*, as a single mother who works full-time, is, I would hazard to guess, very different to the vision of those parents who are at their children's school so often that they are on first name terms with all staff and have their own coffee mug hanging in the staff room. Yes, I want to be involved; no, I cannot actually attend the school. So where does that leave those like me?

Many pay lip service to the adage that 'parents are a child's primary and enduring educators', yet, despite the universal acceptance of the significant difference that a parent can make in a child's education, parent partnership remains a term without an appended hymn sheet for us all to sing from. In this sense, the term becomes very similar to Dahlberg et al.'s (2013) discussion about the term 'quality', where he and his co-authors suggest that a lack of universal definition of the word, despite its prevalent use, basically renders it meaningless. The same authors also refer to Readings' (1999) description of the term 'excellence', where he explains that the word is so generally applied that it is devoid of meaning. The extensive use of terminology such as this creates a culture of acceptance, so that any absence of clear, shared meaning goes unquestioned; instead, we each attribute our own understanding. As a result, we individually act under the mistaken assumption that ours is a definition that is shared. This can, and does, inevitably, cause problems as we approach relationships with firm yet varying expectations of one another, rather than a mutual vision for co-production with parents and how we should go about doing it.

An uncritical acceptance of parent partnership as a term is reflected in education policy. Parents becoming more involved in their child's education is not a recent development, although it has gathered momentum over the last few decades. Within the UK, the *Early Years Foundation Stage* (EYFS, DfE, 2021) makes clear that working in partnership with parents is a statutory requirement for all Early Years settings. It goes on to reiterate this point no less than 60 times; some of these mentions even indicate specific points at which an exchange of information between parents and practitioners is *required* (yes, you've guessed it, predominantly when reporting assessments). However, completely absent from the same document is a definition of what is meant by the term 'parent partnership'. As a result, anything from a tick-box, biannual survey, to the meaningful involvement of parents within curriculum development processes, can all come under the umbrella of this 'partnership'. It is worth noting here that when the Department for Education identifies *who* theEYFS has been developed for it *excludes* parents … just saying.

After the early years, parents appear to fade quite quickly from the policy picture. When children in the UK reach the grand old age of seven, and the EYFS is replaced by the National Curriculum, the term 'parents' becomes no more than a tricky word that Year 2 children need to learn to spell; and when they reach secondary age, well, the curriculum appears to have lost sight of parents entirely. Ofsted noted this void in its 2011 report called *Schools and Parents*. This document observed that opportunities for parental engagement appeared to trail off as children move through the school phases, stating that in secondary school parents had far less understanding of what their children were learning due to a lack of collaboration between parents and teachers. Yet parents' *support* of the education system is expected to remain steadfast. Any parent who has experienced the shock of the Year 6 to Year 7 transition in the UK, will be aware of the extent of the recalibration that is needed, moving from that quick chat with the teacher about how 'little petal may not seem herself today because she was sick in the night' to rarely laying eyes on the elusive and aloof species of 'teacher'. That is, of course, apart from the annual humiliation of the good-old parents' evening merry-go-round, where your child gets criticised in front of a whole audience of other parents pretending not to hear. Ah, parent partnership at its best. Communication ceases as the child gets older, but the parents' concern for their child does not. And for this reason, there are lessons to be learned through reading this book, for practitioners working in all categories of the education and care systems.

SO, WHERE DO WE START?

Let's start with this: overall, the concepts of parent partnership that are introduced through policy are sound. Absolutely, yes, parents should have the opportunity to be more involved in their children's education if they wish, but the problem is that educationalists have now moulded that 'parent' into a generic form that is useful for them. And yet, just like children, we parents are all different. Stand me next to your Earth Mother and you will not find one similarity. Yet policy has envisioned the 'good parent'; the docile recipient of instructions who has unlimited time to do as bidden. And most of us do conform, to the extent that we are able. We obediently write in reading records, we complete homework tasks, we gather ingredients, we cobble together costumes (these were always seriously below par in my case) even if it is done through gritted teeth at the end of a long and exhausting day. We do not do it because we want to do it, or because we see it as a valuable opportunity for our child, we do it because we fear the consequences for our child if we do not. We fear that our child will be *punished for our lack of compliance*. We fear that our child will miss out, be humiliated, will be seen to 'fail' because of us. But is this really what being *involved* in our child's education looks like? Is this co-production? Does this really bear any resemblance to any of our interpretations of what 'parent partnership' means?

REFLECTION POINT

This is a really good point to stop and consider what your relationship with the parents of the children in *your* class/room/setting 'looks' like. Is it a genuine dialogue where information and ideas are passed both ways? Or is it didactic? Do you welcome questions, ideas, or alternative viewpoints? Or would such questioning be seen as 'troublesome'? (Be honest here!) Are you aware which of your parents would enjoy carrying out school tasks with or for their children and those parents that would find it extremely difficult? How well do you actually know these parents and what is going on in their lives?

As well as the unequal power dynamics, with teachers holding all the aces, another sticking point is that the concept of 'parent partnership' was developed at a time when policy-makers were still of the antiquated opinion that the man was the breadwinner and the woman's place was in the home (Lewis and West, 2016). It was not developed with working parents, parents who are carers, single parents, or parents struggling with their own physical or mental health issues, in mind. It was based upon an ideal that is very far removed from the reality of the single-sex parents, stepfamilies, extended families, kinship carers, and many other versions of 'family' that we now interact with day to day. The government has designed just one traditional, round hole that we are attempting to hammer square, rectangular, triangular, even star-shaped pegs into.

The main premise of this book is that you consider parents as individuals with their own hopes, dreams, and aspirations for their child. Because of this we have avoided an approach that says 'this is what you must do with ethnic minority families' or 'this is what you must do with migrant families'. No two families are the same and although we have highlighted, for example, some of the particular struggles experienced by those in poverty, or those who have a child with complex needs, our aim is not for you to see 'groups of people' but to see individuals. To see past skin colour, accents, tattoos, or choice of clothing, to the person who loves that child more than anyone else and is trying to raise their child in the best way that they can; and who wants what is best for them. Even when that parent's actions or choices may not quite fit with the very specific mould of good parent that the education system has created.

As you read this book, we hope that you will take the time to consider what you expect from parent partnerships in your own educational context. To contemplate whether you and the parents that you work with share the same goals, the same aspirations for the child. (And please do note that throughout this book 'parent' means anyone who has taken on a caring role for the child; the biological relationship is irrelevant. The same goes for families – simply those in the caring role in the home.) When nursery leaders spoke with me about the conflicts that sometimes arose with parents, one head teacher explained that it was easy, really, to get back on track, it was simply about the "non-negotiable of holding the needs of children in mind" (Solvason, Webb, and Sutton-Tsang, 2020, p.8). But educationalists need to be more aware that there are times when they should *not* add to the high-anxiety environment of the family home (struggling, perhaps, through an acrimonious divorce, domestic abuse, bereavement, or any difficult time) by making additional demands on the parent. Sometimes *what is best for the child*, is for the educationalist to kerb all demands on that family for the time being, and better still, that they find a ten-minute space for that parent to share their worries about protecting their child through their current, challenging situation. *Always* the best approach is to listen to parents and to find out what is needed. But how often do we really do that with the parents that we work with?

Although the topics do overlap and intertwine, you will be best reading this book from start to finish, as we do our best not to repeat areas that have been discussed before. But if it's 'dipping in and out' or nothing, then please, dip away. Throughout this book we ask you to reflect on how your own practice might be received by the families that you work with and how effectively you nurture these crucial relationships. We really hope that this reflection brings about positive change for you, but we acknowledge that this process is not always a comfortable one. We are asking you to hold on to your knowledge 'lightly' as McNiff (2010) puts it, to interrogate your everyday practice and question your most basic assumptions, becoming aware of influences which may impact these. We are asking you to be open to the possibility that the opinions that you currently hold may need to be reassessed. And we are aware that this may not be easy for you.

For many of us we reflect only as a knee-jerk response when things go *wrong*. Because of that, we connect reflection to professional inadequacy, which makes it reactive in nature, driven only by a fear of failure (Appleby and Hanson, 2017). This does not need to be the case, reflection should not be viewed simply as a 'well maybe we can learn from this' consolation prize for failure, but instead it should be viewed as a process of empowerment and self-efficacy as you hone in on your core values and refocus your practice in light of these. Having said this, the 'mental unrest' that reflective practice requires, as you hold yourself in a place of not yet knowing, is not always easy to deal with. Remember, this is the position that the children who we teach every day sit in much of the time, because we, as educationalists, know that this is where meaningful learning takes place. We urge you to see the benefit in these uncomfortable moments as you become deeply and sincerely curious about the taken-for-granted elements of your practice and, in turn, about the children and families you work with.

We advise you to find a willing ear to talk through these ideas with. (If your partner starts to glaze over mid-sentence, perhaps find an alternative victim.) Share your emerging thoughts with colleagues. Better still, you may have a whole platoon of team-mates who recognise that there is room for development in your setting's parent partnership practice, and you may be looking to make changes on a larger scale. How fantastic would that be? This book provides you the tools that can help you to do that.

We sincerely hope that as you read this book you will begin to consider the parents and the families that you work with in a different light. That you will come to respect and even to enjoy their oddities, their diversity, and their challenges; that you will increasingly admire and utilise the wide-ranging knowledge and experience that they bring to your setting. We hope that you will arrive at a point where you can genuinely value them as partners, remembering that you are both playing for the same team. And if this book merely affirms the values that you already hold and the practice that you already carry out, then fantastic, keep up the good work and spread the word.

TEAM ACTIVITY

Before We Start …

When we are looking to make changes, it is good to have a clear starting point, so I'd like you to start with an 'audit'. Make this as formal and detailed or as ad hoc as you like, it's the reflection bit that is important …

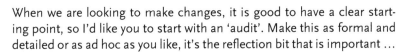

1. Take a walk around your setting (okay, if you are a childminder this may not be overly enlightening) from the entrance hall to the classrooms, and any other shared spaces that you have. Whilst you do so, try to look at your setting through the eyes of a parent. How welcome do you feel? How much evidence can you see that you (as a parent) are a valued part of your child's education?
2. Find any setting policies that make some reference to working with parents. What messages do they convey? What expectations of parents do they project?
3. Try to dig out the last few letters (okay, I'll get with the times, emails, texts, whatever format they might take) that went out to parents. What were they saying? Were they informing, celebrating, requesting, instructing? Again, consider these from a parent's perspective.
4. Finally, consider the last few times that parents were invited into the school. What did parents do when they came in? What arrangements were made to ensure that all parents (including those with full-time work and caring responsibilities) could be included?

WHAT ARE YOUR THOUGHTS AT THIS POINT?

If you were to mark yourself on a scale right now, somewhere between 'we do little more than give our parents information and instructions' and 'we listen to parents and their knowledge and experience fully informs our practice', where do you think you would be?

It's good to know where you are starting so that later on you can appreciate the distance you have covered.

REFERENCES

Appleby, K. and Hanson, K. (2017). Becoming a critically reflective thinker and learner. In Musgrave, M., Savin-Baden, M., and Stobbs, N. (eds). *Studying for Your Early Years Degree*. St Albans: Critical Publishing.

Ball, S.J. (2006). *Education policy and social class: the selected works of Stephen J. Ball.* London: Routledge.

Dahlberg, G., Pence, A.R. and Moss, P. (2013). *Beyond quality in early childhood education and care: languages of evaluation* (3rd ed.). London: Routledge.

Department for Education (2021). *Early years foundation stage.* London: HMSO.

Lewis, J. and West, A. (2016). Early childhood education and care in England under austerity: continuity or change in political ideas, policy goals, availability, affordability and quality in a childcare market? *Journal of Social Policy.* Available from: http://eprints.lse.ac.uk/67492/.

McNiff, J. (2010). *Action research for professional development.* Poole: September Books.

Ofsted (2011). *Schools and parents.* Available from: Ofsted publication, publishing.service.gov.uk.

Readings, B. (1999). *The University in Ruins.* Cambridge, MA: Harvard University Press.

Solvason, C., Webb, R. and Sutton-Tsang, S. (2020). What is left...?: the implications of losing maintained nursery schools for vulnerable children and families in England. *Children and Society.* Available from: https://authorservices.wiley.com/api/pdf/fullArticle/16752045.

CHAPTER 1
Always Listen

Carla Solvason

> *We pride ourselves on our positive parent partnerships at our setting. This has led to parents feeling they can share their worries and concerns, leading to a variety of early interventions and sign-posting to a wide range of advice and support. All leading to alleviation of worry and stress which would otherwise have a detrimental effect on our children.*
>
> *... they just want someone that will listen to them; that will take them seriously, rather than just being fobbed off.*
>
> *Maintained Nursery School Leaders in Solvason, Webb, and Sutton-Tsang (2020a)*

When I interviewed several nursery school leaders (including the two above) about their relationship with parents one of them said "you always listen, you never don't hear" and this phrase really stuck with me. Talking with parents is not about a set of instructions for them, it is about authentically listening. An authentic partnership involves respecting parents' knowledge and seeking their approval for the choices made about their own child, allowing them to retain a sense of control. But obviously we need to consider practical ways that we can do that within a busy working day where every minute is accounted for. Listening means acknowledging the needs of the parents and reconciling these with the perceived needs of the child. How can we, as educationalists, navigate the judgements and expectations on both sides? How can we establish and maintain communication with parents, including those who we are less likely to see during an average school day? In this chapter we will consider some approaches. But first, (just for a change I hear you sigh), a bit about me ....

DOI: 10.4324/9781003191209-1

Just recently I visited my dentist where the receptionist enquired, very loudly through the anti-Covid plexiglass window, whether there had been any significant changes in my health and medication needs since my last visit. Yes, there had been some quite considerable medical events, but I'd be damned if I was going to announce those to the waiting room full of people all pretending not to listen (really, what else is there to do when all of the gossip magazines have all been removed? I'd be doing the same). So, of course, I answered "no". It was a barefaced lie, but this was neither the time nor the place to have that discussion and frankly the receptionist was totally insane to expect otherwise, had she even heard of data protection? This wholly uncomfortable situation made me reflect on the type of information that we expect from parents and the ways that we go about obtaining it.

For some, the parents' evening carousel, ensuring glorification for the parents of over-achievers (smug lot) and humiliation for the likes of me, is the only chance that parents have to interact with teachers. And all in front of a room packed with other parents, a non-paying audience pretending (just like in the waiting room) not to be listening. Of course, the parents of troublesome children do get more opportunity for interaction outside of parents evening. I can say with all honesty that 99% of any personalised communication coming from my boys' school was because the teachers wanted to let me know that my children had failed to comply (messing about, failing to complete homework, you know, the normal stuff ... they didn't set the school on fire or anything, at least I'm not aware that they did) and they wanted me to do a better job *of making them toe the line*. I had to 'back them up', regardless of whether I actually agreed with the reasons or fairness of the situation. This was my experience of "co-production' during my boys' secondary schooling. I sincerely hope that this is not the norm.

THE REASONS FOR WORKING WITH PARENTS: THE IDEAL

A research report in 2009 (by Sherbert Research) discussed how the most effective engagement with parents involved affirmation, empowerment, reassurance, and support. How fantastic would it be if this were the basis of all parent–educator relationships? If we, as practitioners were able to nurture the families that we work with in the same way that we nurture their children? But for most of us this is an ideal that remains firmly out of reach. Posey-Maddox and Haley-Lock (2020, p.694) discussed how, in their research, they found that although "strong family–school relationships" were commonly seen as a hugely influential factor in the student's success, the reality was that these were simply another "add-on" to the roles and responsibilities of the harried educator. Likewise, Chan and Ritchie (2016, p.290) discuss the fact that "Whilst official documents … espouse the notion of 'partnership with parents', the application of this in practice appears to be uneven".

In most cases I would argue that it's not so much that educators don't *want to* develop meaningful relationships with parents, more that they simply *can't* achieve this successfully in their already overly-burdened teaching day. Argyris and Schön (1974) refer to this as an individual's espoused theory as opposed to their theory in action. Your espoused theory is that which you believe is right, the values that you hold, and which will form the basis of discussions with others. In contrast to this, your theory in action is what you are actually *able* to do within the limits of your working day. So, for example, you know how important it is to acknowledge all of the parents in the morning, but your TA is off sick, and you just have to get this equipment ready before the students come in, so you simply can't. Or, when your own ideas about children managing their behaviour do not align with the awards and sanctions policy of your current setting. Argyris and Schön (1974) found that there was often quite a wide gap between what we value and how we actually act, which I am sure we can all relate to.

REFLECTION POINT

If you were able to paint a picture of the 'ideal' relationship between yourself and the parents of the children that you care for right now, what would that look like?

We are all familiar with the reams of research, from Vygotsky (1978) through to Callanan et al. (2017), that explains to us how important an influence parents can be upon their child's educational attainment; but there is so much more to consider that just improved grades. During our conversations with nursery leaders their primary focus was the wellbeing of the child. They stressed that without the child feeling *safe* they would be in no position to learn, just as a lack of food or a lack of sleep would prevent them from being able to engage. Their primary aim, therefore, was to work side-by-side with the families to make sure that these basic needs were being met first, and then the learning could come after. This is why these practitioners became involved in helping parents to sort out housing, or finances, or access to foodbanks. Their theory was that happy parents equalled happy children ready to learn.

> I'm pretty certain that those in the early years will be, but are you all aware of Maslow's hierarchy of needs? This is a psychological theory dating from the 1940s that suggests that basic physiological and safety needs of humans must be attended to before they can be motivated to pay attention to learning in new ways.

But beyond learning or being ready to learn, listening to parents is also vitally important from a safeguarding point of view. In our conversations with leaders, they discussed how important it was to be aware when 'the wheels were getting wobbly' in families and being able to step in. They explained:

> *We're a prevention, rather than a cure. I mean, we have these very hard cases, child protection cases and the kids get taken off them, and they need to. But just before that, is that bit where you're coming up to the cliff, and you haven't quite jumped off? Yeah, because of the relationships, you can stop that jumping off the cliff.*

Now I'm not suggesting for one minute that you all have the responsibility to act as educator, family support worker, and safeguarding officer all rolled into one, I'm simply suggesting that you take an interest in the lives of the families that you work with and keep your ears and eyes open for warning signs that problems may be brewing, with the safety of the child in mind. Always listen. Laming's 2003 recount of the tragically neglected and abused Victoria Climbié and, unfortunately, many reports since, remind us that we all have an active role to play in the wellbeing of the children who we work with, and we cannot do this effectively without finding the space to listen to their parents.

THE PROBLEM

So, what is it that stops us from listening? I shall get on to the more obvious problem of time, shortly, but first it is important to look at your setting's culture. In a publication that we wrote in 2019, Johanna and I (along with our colleague Emma) discussed how the educational system silences parents. "But we do listen to our parents, we have satisfaction surveys and all sorts" I hear you cry. The problem is that these tokenistic approaches are usually based upon the needs of the setting, and what the setting views the responsibilities and priorities of 'a good parent' as being. They are also, if we are brutally honest, often about getting parents to do what we need them to do to improve pupil attainment. Posey-Maddox and Haley-Lock joined the debate in 2020, stressing that their research was based upon "previous studies that have identified the need to move beyond school-centric, teacher-driven models of parent involvement" (p.694). They emphasise that we should start with the needs of the parent, rather than what we, as a setting, need from them. And in doing so, that we should "craft opportunities for engagement tailored to families' unique life contexts and assets" (Posey-Maddox and Haley-Lock, 2020, p.673).

Then there's the time aspect. I know, there are so many other priorities. But let me just say this; in my work with nurseries where relationships with parents and the wellbeing of the family were prioritised, they were working in areas of extreme deprivation. This meant that many children were entering the nursery way behind on their development goals and with multiple needs. Yet almost all the children left the nursery at the expected level of development. It's good to bear this, and Maslow (1943) in mind when deciding what we need to prioritise from a range of possible options.

5

Now, I know what you are thinking, it's a bit like policy, this all well and good but how the blazes do you actually implement it? Well, let me give you some real-life experience from my previous research rather than just a list of airy-fairy ideas. In the following discussion I make frequent reference to research carried out with Maintained Nursery Schools (MNS), with my wonderful colleagues Rebecca Webb and Sam Sutton-Tsang, which was published in 2020 (a and b) and to the research that the inspirational Sam Proctor and I carried out with teachers in a special educational needs (SEN) school, published in 2021. These projects, and the inspiring people that I've had the pleasure to work with, have helped form the basis of my understanding of what 'good parent partnership' looks like. For ease in this section, I shall refer to these projects as the MNS research and SEN research, but the full references are found in the list at the end of this chapter.

REFLECTION POINT

First consider this:

Do you have someone who is always available to talk to parents should they have concerns? Many leaders glibly use the phrase 'my door is always open' but what does that look like in practice?
How accessible is a listening ear to those parents who work long hours?
How welcoming is the space (actual or virtual)?
How are parents put at ease?
Is there any privacy for what may well be difficult conversations?

AN 'OPEN DOOR'

In my research with maintained nursery schools one leader said this:

[Being here] ... over many generations means that the MNS is a place of safety and reputation. When families are experiencing

6

things they come back here, even when their children have left because they think, "I know I'll be listened to. I know somebody will help me here".

Now, this may seem a little extreme, I mean, it's hard enough to find time for current students' parents, right? But what does this say about the type of relationship that this setting had created with its parents and local community? I would argue that it speaks volumes. Much of the strength of the relationships that these nurseries built with parents came from a culture of authentic care, but another prevalent quality was consistency. Several leaders commented on the fact that if you let parents down just once then any trust previously built will be broken. Trust is so very important, and so very fragile, as Johanna discusses in the next chapter. This MNS leader stressed:

I think it's about your reliability … you have to be utterly reliable to exactly what you're going to do, and you always do it consistently. And you operate together within the team, so that you don't get one response from one person and a different response from somebody else. … You can manage it in different ways, if it's not the best time to, you know you haven't got the staffing to be able to sit with somebody, you manage that in another way, but parents have to be able to rely, because if you if you get it wrong, once, actually, you've blown it. You know what I mean? You have to be utterly consistent.

Another leader discussed how her office was at the heart of the school and accessible to all, at any time. This is great for those parents who are able to actually make it into the school during the working day, but what about those parents that Oostdam and Hooge (2013, p.344) refer to as 'invisible'? Those who are never 'present', never available for school trips or parents' evenings? Well, there are two different issues here, those parents who, perhaps, simply feel uncomfortable at the school, and those who are unable to make it due to work and other commitments. Or actually, reflecting on my own situation it was my inability to be 'present' at the school which led to me feeling judged, which led to me feeling uncomfortable at the school. So sometimes it may not be that clear cut. But still, let's consider each of these aspects in turn, and look at some ideas to navigate them.

TACKLING DISCOMFORT

One leader at an MNS school took a 'Muhammad and the mountain' approach to this. For the 'drop and run' parents (okay, my hand's up, who else?) she would go out to the car park to meet them. Just those seeds of human contact are often all that is needed for trust to begin to grow. Even the least confident and most shy parents will have times that they do not want to feel alone in their struggles (Brown and Isaacs, 2005) so sometimes it is finding kind ways to gently break down those barriers. For parents who are already stressed, attending a session on "improving your child's literacy" may be a step too far, but a child-friendly session on "Parent Wellness" and "Self-Compassion: Taking care of ourselves so we can keep being great parents" (ibid., p.87) may be just the ticket. Especially if held in an evening, or on a weekend. Opportunities like this can also give you a 'heads up' in terms of those who make the effort to attend, and what that might tell you about their current wellbeing.

Another way to build bridges is to hold school events in community locations, so that parents and educators can interact on more familiar ground for the families. For educators this may mean stepping into spaces that feel uncomfortable. Places that are dominated by a very different culture to the school, places that may represent different ethnicities and different religions, but remember that those families make that step into somewhere unfamiliar every day. And what about activities on weekends and outside of school hours to enable working parents to attend? One MNS setting held parent and child cookery classes on the weekend, which turned out to be a particularly successful way to get parents through the door. Now, no one wants to work a six-day week, so this is a management issue. If you were to host similar sessions how could time given outside of school hours be recompensed during the week? Go on – ask your boss their thoughts on this.

In one nursery that I spoke with they took their children to the local old people's home. The children took playdough and made beautiful creations (at least from a *really* long distance away) with the residents there. As well as forging trusting relationships between the nursery and the community this also had some more tangible benefits. The manipulation of the playdough was extremely effective in exercising arthritic hands, and the children benefitted from one-to-one conversations with an interested adult, developing their language and their confidence. Simple but effective. Let's do more activities like this.

In their work with SEN children, Sam and his colleagues would frequently have parents that they had never actually met face to face, due to children being transported into the setting from some distance away. In these cases, they would make regular use of a quick telephone chat to maintain contact. And in terms of the very specific needs of SEN children this contact was vital because, as Sedibe and Fourie (2018, p.433) rationalise: "Parents take up the role of primary teachers at the conception of their children and this lifelong commitment makes them experts with respect to the needs of their children". One of the teachers of SEN children explained it this way during our research:

> We need the context of, how their weekend was, how they were this morning, things that might potentially be problematic during the day that we need to be aware of. It's just important to get the whole wider picture, otherwise we're guessing all day. If the family can just tell us "oh this can be because of … x,y,z" then it stops us from trying to guess.

It is important to point out that this dialogue did not only relate to the youngest children, this SEN school caters for children aged from four to 16. It is a shame that the value of dialogue with the parents of children with SEN is recognised regardless of the child's age, but that the continuation of an ongoing dialogue, throughout the child's challenging teenaged years, is not often maintained in mainstream schooling.

In our post-pandemic culture communication at a distance has become the norm rather than the exception. But let us not forget the importance of human contact. Although messaging and shared websites are 'low stakes' ways of maintaining contact with parents, the five minutes sat beside a parent showing them how to use a platform is invaluable. Instead of a text message send a voice message. Whenever possible personalise your interaction with parents so that they feel seen and valued (Rubin et al., 2012).

NOT JUDGING

I mentioned above that I felt judged for being "an absent mother" at my sons' school, concerned that my absenteeism would be interpreted as a lack of care. This wasn't paranoia, it was because I worked with teachers, so I knew exactly how I would be perceived. The same is found in literature worldwide. Writing in New Zealand, Chan and Ritchie (2016, p.291) comment that "Unfortunately, some teachers assume that parents who are not present within the learning settings are uninvolved and/or disinterested in their children's education". And I think that 'some teachers' here is generous, it's more than likely most. We, as educators, tend not to think beyond the walls of our setting and can fail to recognise the wealth of cultural learning that could be taking place in family homes and communities (Posey-Maddox and Haley-Lock, 2020, p.673). How wonderful if we could harness more of that colour and diversity in the experiences of our children? Remember we only provide one aspect of what a child needs to develop into a fully rounded individual, many other adults input into a child's holistic development. Let's find out more about our families, their culture, and their traditions, and seek to use these to widen the experience of all of the children in our care.

REFLECTION POINT

Consider the culture of your setting as objectively as you are able. Is it welcoming for *all* parents that enter? Are they made to feel that they belong? If so, how? Or is it a closed or a threatening environment where individuals fear they will be judged?

The Sherbert Research (2009, p.5) concluded that often those parents perceived as *hard to reach* "prioritise their children's wellbeing and happiness over academic achievement". That was me. Despite being in the education 'business' my view has always been that there is far more to achieving a quality life than getting good grades. Added to the fact that so much of the work set for my children was, quite frankly, meaningless. Why, in the name of all that is holy, should a dyslexic eleven-year-old be given the homework task of copying out four pages of print. What is being achieved here? It is labour, not learning. For those parents who appear more disengaged in their child's learning, the report suggests (ibid.), we need to be passing on "information that reassures, supports, and informs them" and should "demonstrate an understanding of the emotional and practical challenges facing parents, and offer them solutions that meet their own particular needs". Each family is unique and will have its own challenges, but also its own aims, so try to get to know and understand what these are. Similar to the points made earlier, a relationship with parents needs to start with acknowledgement of the parents' needs, not a myopic, or 'school-centric' focus upon the priorities of the school. It needs to see parents as individuals and not as a genus.

One MNS leader stressed the importance of respect for the individual:

> *You know there's a lot of conflict, it's an inner-city area so obviously, there's levels of crime and … there's conflict between people, but it's very rare that that spills over once people have come through the threshold to the nursery school. Because they know, that actually the values of the place, are that each person is recognised and valued and that respectful behaviour is that which is required for our youngest children; that's what we're trying to set as the norm.*

The approach taken by the MNSs that we spoke with was strengths-based. Although acknowledging the challenges of the community it also saw the community as capable of its own regeneration, with the needs of its children as a focus. For example, a parent losing their job was turned into the positive that they would be able to come and spend more time in the setting. This is similar to Brown and Isaacs's (2005) concept of a 'World Café conversation' where the assumption is "that communities have within them the wisdom and creativity to confront even the most difficult challenges". Of course, maintaining common ground across micro-communities that might be quite different can be quite tough, as this MNS leader explained:

> *I mean, don't get me wrong. We get shouted at; we get sworn at. We are just real with them. I say to them, come on, you're obviously very angry. But I don't think we need to be like this. Come on, let's calm down and sort it out.*

But key here is the 'we', a sharing of responsibility, co-construction of the child's educational experience, an attitude that says we will sort it out *together*.

I am not sure how many of you will be familiar with Bronfenbrenner's ecological theory (1974) but it is relevant here. This theory acknowledges that the child is impacted upon by their relationship with the world around them. They are most affected by their immediate experiences in the spheres of their homelife and their school day, these are their micro-systems. They are also influenced, albeit more indirectly, by the sociocultural dynamics of their wider community, which might include factors such as religious traditions and beliefs, these are known as their exo-systems. Finally, they are influenced by those that they don't even see, such as politicians and those developing nationwide policy, and this is called their macro-system. Between these different systems are the meso-systems, where interaction takes place; so, for example, your communication with parents takes place in the meso-system between home and school.

The reason I mention this is because difficulties can arise for the child when there is a mismatch in their different spheres of experience. As Soule and Curtis (2021, p.134) explain, "Each microsystem functions differently, and children learn to adapt to expected routines, rules, and rhythms of home, a classroom, or a community"; importantly they add that "Tension and conflicts can arise when expectations and norms vary in the meso-system". It is reaching an equilibrium and a shared understanding in this meso-system that is key for us as educators working with parents.

REFLECTION POINT

In the playground you notice a parent of one of the children in your class disciplining their child in a way that is poles apart from the school policy and from what you believe to be good practice. What do you do? You have a range of options:

You could be brave and confront the parent, explaining why their behaviour is inappropriate.

You could send a (passive aggressive) newsletter home informing parents of the approaches taken to behaviour management in school and what might be useful for them to try at home.

Or you could simply open up a conversation with the parent. Ask how they are doing. Ask how they are finding managing their child's behaviour, anything in particular that they find difficult. You could ask if there is anything that they find helpful when dealing with their child's behaviour. And finally, you could share some approaches that you use that you have found really helpful in the classroom.

Only one of these approaches bears any resemblance to a dialogue and a partnership.

What is important to remember in situations where conflicts arise is that there is not one approach that is 'right' and one that is 'wrong'. Ways of doing things can vary from classroom to classroom let alone between the classroom and home; the important thing is to step into the issue and discuss ways of moving forward more synchronously, for the wellbeing of the child. As Pavlakis (2018, p.1067) advises, "schools need to create spaces to learn from … families. By creating these spaces, schools may also foster trust and share power with families". For this to happen we need to aim to enter into genuine dialogue with parents where ideas and solutions are co-constructed, and not just give a stream of instructions.

SITTING BESIDE

In the introduction to this book, and in Johanna's chapter later (Chapter 4), we discuss how emotionally challenging parenting can be. Orphan (2004, p.98) refers to feelings that never existed before, such as "uncontrollable rage, sorrow or a deep sense of joy" that can emerge after having children – and to the fact that Britain is "a society that is not very good at managing feeling" (p.106). I'm sure that all Brits will (quietly and rationally, of course) agree with that. But the most important point that Orphan (2004, p.98) raises is that although *all* parents can experience highs and lows of emotion that are new to them, "For parents of children with disabilities" those sensations are "even more intense and can be fairly constant". Likewise, Truss (2008, p.375), who described her experience of dealing with a total of 57 different professionals whilst seeking a diagnosis for her son's SEN, stresses the lack of support that exists for parents during a time when their "emotional burden verges on the intolerable". As educators, our experience with SEN will be hugely varied, but it is important that we are aware of the very unique needs of the parents of children with SEN when dealing with them.

One teacher in our SEN research reflected on how parents could "be very, very defensive, quite angry sometimes, very frustrated" when they first arrived at their school; but, critically, she added, "You just have to remember all that rubbish that they've been through: and be kind to them". The teachers in the specialist school shared how they spent a great deal of time reassuring parents who had continually heard only negatives about their child for a very long time as they went through the statementing process. It is really helpful to remember that a child must be seen to fail again, and again, and again to obtain a statement; and hearing continual negatives about their child can be soul destroying for a parent. Because of this the SEN teachers that we interviewed went to great lengths to share positive comments with parents just to break the cycle of negativity that they had previously experienced. A simple "they did this today! It was really good, it was, you know, they were amazing" was shared as often as possible to reassure parents that at this school their child would be just fine.

REFLECTION POINT

A parent in Wolfendale's 2013 research commented that if parents felt that the teacher genuinely cared about the child, then their relationship was "made". Why might this be the case and what are your thoughts on this? In what ways do you demonstrate "genuine care" to the children that you work with?

As both an educator and a human being it is the small things that can make a huge difference in our interactions with others. An MNS leader described how when she saw a parent arrive at the setting "in a ratty mood" she would say something positive about their child to cheer them up. Because, she added, it was easy to do that. Another leader explained her experience of "being there" for parents, she said: "we were there along the way. And it might have just been a smile in the morning or a hug in the afternoon. A 'Come on, let's go and get a cup of tea'. Let's go. What can I do?". All practitioners commented on the significant difference these small moments of kindness, of sitting beside parents, could make.

WAYS FORWARD

Georgis et al. (2014) suggest that inclusive parent partnership incorporates four key features, and I would like you to consider these:

1. Parent engagement should be reciprocal, the role of parents is not simply to fulfil school requests.
2. Parent engagement is just like any relationship, trust needs to be there for parents to feel comfortable to speak and for them to be heard.
3. Parent engagement needs to be aware of and respond to cultural and linguistic difference.
4. Parent engagement should mirror our relationship with their children, responding to need and encompassing strengths.

These are really useful starting points for us at this juncture.

I am a firm believer in regular contact between parents and educators and parents' presence (or voice) at the school not being 'an event' but the norm. In this way any issues can be tackled as they arise, they do not have time to fester. Inviting parents into the classrooms and workshops is an easy way to do this, but let's focus on the 'invisible parents' who are not around during the working day. One approach to this would be to have an 'open classroom' one evening a month, for parents who would like to pop in and chat, or even on a Saturday morning. I realise that this may seem like getting blood from a stone where educationalists are concerned, on top of a jam-packed working week, but it could eliminate many of the minor niggles which can take up hours of the working day. (And, again, it would be up to your boss to sort out the equity of this in terms of hours … an afternoon or morning off to recompense?) It goes without saying that this would be invaluable to those parents unable to attend school during the working day, who are missing those brief information-sharing moments with their child's teacher.

CONCLUSION

Now, I know we are not 'teaching' parents, but I would just like to use an example from my interaction with students to demonstrate the importance of personalised communication. I teach students in the final year of their Bachelor of Arts degree at university, a point in their studies where they should know referencing like the back of their hand, be adept at planning assignments and understand how to incorporate criticality into their writing. That's the theory. Because, in reality, there remains plenty of room for development with these areas I teach 'refresher sessions on them, I produce helpful Powerpoints and I send reminder emails of key points; but nothing seems to make any significant difference. After the students had submitted a particularly disappointing piece of written work, I arranged to meet with them all face-to-face, one-to-one, to talk through their writing. Every one of them said how useful the conversation was and that they now understood where they were going wrong. I wasn't saying anything different to the same things that I had said repeatedly in the whole group sessions, but this time it was personal to them, and they felt comfortable seeking clarification on points that remained a little murky to them. Making time for personalised interaction with parents is a sacrifice, and something that you could perfectly legitimately avoid in your busy days, but it is also invaluable.

Chan and Ritchie (2016, p.292) tell us that:

> parent–teacher partnership involves a trusting, respectful relationship, two-way communication, collaboration, empowerment, equal power and shared decision-making, rather than parents being "advised" about how to rear their children or expected to conform to the teachers' expectations.

Let's bear these ideas of a dialogue and authentic co-construction in mind as we tackle the other areas of this book.

KEY POINTS TO TAKE AWAY FROM THIS CHAPTER

1. The potential benefits *for the child* of working more closely with parents. Or 'happy parents equal happy children'.
2. The narrow view of a 'good parent' that our educational system has created. What are your 'expectations' of parents in your setting? Do you see parents as individuals?
3. The importance of understanding where parents are 'coming from' – what has been their experience with settings before this point?
4. Valuing (and showing that you value) the information that parents give.
5. Providing an appropriate environment to speak with parents, making them feel welcome and respecting their privacy.
6. Respecting the values, aims, and priorities of each family.
7. Recognising the wisdom and experience to be found within families and communities and respecting (and where possible incorporating) this within the setting.

TEAM ACTIVITY

What Type of Setting Do You Want to Be?

Oostdam and Hooge (2013, p.346) emphasise how important it is for settings to identify realistic aims for themselves in terms of the type of setting that they would like, and are able to be. They set out the following options:

1) Information-oriented setting: this type of setting focuses on providing accurate information to parents. Most contact with parents is formal and based upon providing information.

2) Structure-oriented setting: in addition to providing accurate information this type of setting also likes to establish clear structures. Within such a setting the tasks and responsibilities of parents and the setting are clearly set out and contact with parents remains strictly in accordance with procedure.

3) Relation-oriented setting: this setting, like those above, focuses on accurate information and clear structures, but it also aims to develop relationships with parents. There is a conscious effort to develop and maintain individual contact with parents.

4) Participation-oriented setting: this setting does all of the above, but also focuses upon developing parent participation. The setting proactively seeks out contact with parents and aims to actively involve parents in all aspects of education.

5) Innovation-oriented setting: the difference with this approach to that above is that parents are not recipients but equals, both take a proactive approach. In such a setting, parents are active partners in the continual improvement of education experiences and the educational environment.

Which of the options above enable quality of access and experience for all?

Where are you now as a setting and where would you like to be?

What changes might you need to put in place to enable that?

REFERENCES

Argyris, C. and Schön, D. (1974). *Theory in practice: increasing professional effectiveness*. San Francisco, CA: Jossey-Bass.

Bronfenbrenner, U. (1974). Developmental research, public policy, and the ecology of childhood. *Child Development*, 45(1), 1–5.

Brown, J. and Isaacs, D. (2005). *The world café: shaping our futures through conversations that matter*. San Francisco, CA: Berrett-Koehler.

Callanan, M., Anderson, M., Haywood, S., Hudson, R. and Speight, S. (2017). *Study of early education and development*. Research Report. Available from: https://assets.publishing.service.gov.uk/government/uploads/system/uploads/attachment_data/file/586242/SEED_ _Good_Practice_in_Early_Education_-_RR553.pdf.

Chan, A. and Ritchie, J. (2016). Parents, participation, partnership: problematising New Zealand early childhood education. *Contemporary Issues in Early Childhood*, 17(3), 289–303.

Georgis, R., Gokiert, R., Ford, D. and Ali, M. (2014). Creating inclusive parent engagement practices: lessons learned from a school community collaborative supporting newcomer refugee families. *Multicultural Education*, 21(3–4), 23–27.

Laming, W.H. (2003). The Victoria Climbie inquiry: report of an inquiry by Lord Laming (Cm. 5730). Available from https://assets.publishing.service.gov.uk/government/uploads/system/uploads/attachment_data /file/273183/5730.pdf.

Maslow, A.H. (1943). A theory of human motivation. *Psychological Review*, 50, 370–396. https://doi.org/10.1037/h0054346.

Oostdam, R. and Hooge, E. (2013). Making the difference with active parenting; forming educational partnerships between parents and schools. *European Journal of the Psychology of Education*, 28, 337–351.

Orphan, A. (2004). *Moving on: supporting parents of children with SEN*. London: Fulton.

Pavlakis, A.E. (2018). Reaching all families: family, school, and community partnerships amid homelessness and high mobility in an urban district. *Urban Education*, 53(8), 1043–1073.

Posey-Maddox, L. and Haley-Lock, A. (2020). One size does not fit all: understanding parent engagement in the contexts of work, family, and public schooling. *Urban Education*, 55(5), 671–698.

Rubin, C.L., Martinez, L.S., Chu, J., Hacker, K., Brugge, D., Pirie, A., Allukian, N., Rodday, A.M. and Leslie, L.K. (2012). Community-engaged pedagogy: a strengths-based approach to involving diverse stakeholders in research partnerships. *Progress in Community Health Partnerships: Research, Education, and Action*, 6(4), 481–490. https://doi.org/10.1353/ cpr.2012.0057.

Sedibe, M. and Fourie, J. (2018). Exploring opportunities and challenges in parent–school partnerships in special needs schools in the Gauteng Province, South Africa. *Interchange*, 49(4), 433–444. https://doi.org/10.1007/s10780-018-9334-5.

Sherbert Research (2009). *Parents as pcartners -'Harder to Engage' parents. Qualitative research on behalf of the DCSF*. Available from: https://dera.ioe.ac.uk/11166/1/DCSF-RR111.pdf.

Solvason, C., Cliffe, J. and Bailey, E. (2019). Breaking the silence: providing authentic opportunities for parents to be heard. *Power and Education*, 11(2), 191–203. https://doi.org/10.1177/1757743819837659.

Solvason, C. and Proctor, S. (2021). 'You have to find the right words to be honest': nurturing relationships between teachers and parents of children with special educational needs. *Support for Learning*, 36(3), 470–485.

Solvason, C., Webb, R. and Sutton-Tsang, S. (2020a). Evidencing the effects of maintained nursery schools' roles in early years sector improvements. Available from: https://tactyc.org.uk/research/.

Solvason, C., Webb, R. and Sutton-Tsang, S. (2020b). What is left...?: the implications of losing maintained nursery schools for vulnerable children and families in England. *Children and Society*. https://authorservices.wiley.com/api/pdf/fullArticle/16752045.

Soule, N.E. and Curtis, H.L. (2021). High school home visits: parent–teacher relationships and student success. *Curtis School Community Journal*, 31(2), 131–153.

Truss, C. (2008). Peter's story: reconceptualising the UK SEN system. *European Journal of Special Needs Education*, 23(4), 365–377. https://doi.org/10.1080/08856250802387349.

Vygotsky, L.S. (1978). *Mind in society: the development of higher psychological processes*. Cambridge, MA: Harvard University Press.

Wolfendale, S. (2013). *Working with parents of children with SEN after the code of practice*. Hoboken, NJ: Taylor and Francis.

CHAPTER 2
Avoid Assumptions

Carla Solvason

We frequently make assumptions about people. We can instantly 'write someone off' by the way that they dress, where they live or the way that they speak. You know ... the child from that family that you (without even realising) lower your aspirations for. The parents with matching Crocs. If you deny it, I won't believe you. I grew up on a 'rough', working-class council estate (as it was then, Housing Association conurbation or whatever it is now). But it was okay, because our estate was a bit posher than the other one, on the other side of the canal, that one was *really* rough. Unfortunately, the other side of the canal is where I went to high school. I played a lot of sports as a teenager, and the more affluent schools, from more respected areas, were terrified of us when it came to matches, I think they expected us to have penknives tucked down our knickers. Yet the reality was that we were a bunch of wimps. Presumptions were made because of the school we went to. (On the other hand, I did almost get trampled to death by a herd of innocent looking cows ... but although vaguely in line with the misconception theme here, that's a different story entirely.)

OTHERING

We have a society that readily embraces stereotypes and nurtures prejudice and fear. In our previous work, Johanna and I discussed how individuals feel happier and more comfortable with 'same' and shun 'other' as something to be feared (Cliffe and Solvason, 2019, 2020). In the same way, our education system has created a generic mould for the acceptable parent. We have a very clear idea

DOI: 10.4324/9781003191209-2

of what a good parent *looks like*. Yet, in reality, parents differ just as much as children in their "dispositions, individual personalities, religion, race and culture, income, socio-economic status, class, health, nationality" (Wilson, 2016, p.6). And when it comes to our interactions with them, it is important to remember that the first two characteristics mentioned by Wilson are significantly more important than the rest of them.

In our educational system the 'good parent' is a specific type of person who acts in very specific ways (Haines Lyon, 2018) and the expectations of schools, or the 'playing field' and 'rules' as Oost-dam and Hooge (2013, p.344) refer to them, are built around that. The traditional school-based model of parental engagement is based upon the types of language used by, and the typical participation practices of, white and middle-class parents (Lawson, 2003). Those that present, or behave, in ways that do not conform to these practices deemed as acceptable, are frequently viewed as 'other'. And 'other', in educational terms is generally a bad thing. And please do not be fooled into thinking that stereotypical perceptions of the 'disinterested' lower-income parent are only restricted to the UK. Chappel and Ratliffe (2021) explored this topic in Hawai'i and found exactly the same; "biased preconceptions" that educators can have concerning disadvantaged families such as the "deficit assumptions that minority and low-income parents place a low value on education". Think carefully about whether, at any point, you have 'bought into' this way of thinking without challenging it. If we are honest, it is likely that most of us have at some point.

THE FAMILY

The 21st-century reality of the family is far more complex than could ever have been imagined a century ago (Wilson, 2016, p.8). The structure of the modern-day family unit is now likely to include all manner of different step-father-mother-sister-brother makeups through divorce, separation, and remarriage; adoptive parental roles; foster parents and kinship carers (including grand-parents, aunts and uncles, and older siblings); stay-at-home fathers and full-time working mothers; single parents and same sex parents … the list goes on. I have even taught a child whose mother and her two male partners lived happily in the same house, and that was over 30 years ago. With the many other diversities mentioned above, and those that have not yet been mentioned, it goes without saying that a one-size-fits-all approach to working with families is just not appropriate and, as Posey-Maddox and Haley-Lock (2020) found through their research in the United States, is likely to have limited success. Yet this image is ingrained within our subconscious, despite the 'catch all' phrase of 'parents or carers', in reality 'mum and dad' is the audience for every registration form, every letter home, every piece of guidance. Should we really still be buying into the marketing of notions such as Mother's Day and Father's Day so wholeheartedly, when in many settings the 'nuclear family' is now the exception rather than the rule?

> Just recently my students and I were discussing the diversity of families, and one student shared how even she, as a lesbian living with her partner, always uses the term 'mum and dad' with the children. Let's get in the habit of saying 'parents' or 'family'.

ENGAGING PARENTS

Within Brooker's (2010) research into partnership working, she identifies that many activities that have become the mainstays, or the best practice approaches to engaging with parents, are not universally applicable or even sound. Very often these tick box, tokenistic activities, that begin as attempts at honouring individual requirements inadvertently become practices that are isolating and potentially silencing. When a questionnaire or a letter goes home, what about the parents who cannot read? What about the parents with English as an additional language? In situations such as these, some families become labelled as *hard to reach* when, in fact, the means taken to contact them have been wholly inappropriate.

Posey-Maddox and Haley-Lock (2020) found this in their research in the US, where efforts to engage parents deemed 'more challenging' actually exacerbated the situation rather than improving it. They identify that a key mistake educators often make is a failure to really *see* the parent, as the complex individual that they are, resulting in "missed opportunities to build upon parents' assets, interests, varied life contexts, and other forms of engagement in the home or broader community" (Posey-Maddox and Haley-Lock, 2020, p.672). Or a failure to access those funds of knowledge found in the family home, as Moll and Greenberg (1990) refer to it. So where are things going wrong? The problem appears to be largely centred upon our failure, as educators, to see, and appreciate parents, as they actually *are*, because we are so preoccupied with our image of what they *should be*. So let's start by being open to viewing things a little differently.

REFLECTION POINT

Be honest with yourself here, what is it that you tend to see as 'red flags' – what things spring to mind? Let's consider some of the stereotypical images that have become part of 'othering' social classes:

The pit bull or similar, aggressive-looking dog. Often viewed as a status symbol, 'real men' (you know, the type that go to the pub most nights for a pint and a fight) have one of these. In reality, these are, on the whole, very loving dogs that are great with children. I used to have a rottweiler that people would cross the road to avoid. If it was a black Labrador or a Chihuahua at the end of the lead would your first impression of that person be the same?

An ample chest on display in low-cut top. Obviously this means a woman is attention seeking, promiscuous. If a slim, athletic-looking woman had the same top on, would your judgement be the same?

Cigarette in hand. Obviously this means *a bit rough*, wasteful with money, unhealthy, dirty. Yet, when we see a cigarette in the hand of the rich and famous, we think none of those things.

A number of my friends, family, and colleagues smoke, and most of those that don't have at some point. Most of my childhood was spent within a fug of smoke thanks to my parents and relatives (rah-rah skirts, perms, and smoking, all staples of the 1980s), yet my mother could give Mrs Bouquet a run for her money in her primness and self-righteousness. Like eating white bread, this has now become something that the *respectable* person would not dream of doing.

Tattoos and piercings. A sign of menace or of fun and creativity? For me, just like dreadlocks or dying your hair, these indicate playfulness, self-expression, daring, they are fun. Sometimes a little ill-judged (that man with the huge spider on his face, I'm talking to you), but certainly nothing ominous. On the other hand, my partner shared with me that he would not employ someone with really visible tattoos (that's me out then!). Clearly, he is still living in the past century.

What are your thoughts on these things? I have tattoos and piercings, I've had an aggressive-looking dog, let's face it, I'd probably wear a low-cut top if I had the chest for it … does that make me a certain type of person? It's easy to make assumptions, it's harder to get to know a person. Challenge yourself not to take the easy way out.

As educators it is easy to form a judgement of parents based on a two-dimensional appraisal of their appearance, their ethnicity, their clothes, their age, or perhaps we make judgements based upon the way that they speak, including their accent, and what that indicates about their intelligence. Cooper (2009, p.381) explains that these factors that we initially observe take no account, whatsoever, of the "the intricacy of parents' lives, demands, schedules, goals, values, and their relationships with their children". And it is that last element that is key to us as educators, their relationship with their children. In the research that I carried out in maintained nursery schools (Solvason, Webb, and Sutton-Tsang, 2020) many of the families were living in poverty and many were isolated. Many struggled financially and emotionally. Yet whilst we can be quick enough to make judgements about 'that parent who can't afford school dinners but is always wearing designer gear', we know nothing about their home life. We often have no idea of the struggles that these families are enduring.

LET'S START WITH FOOD …

Okay, it may seem a little random, but considering assumptions it's as good a place to start as any. One nursery leader told me the story of a mother who collapsed from hunger whilst dropping her child off at the setting. One of the staff drove her to a foodbank. It is with this in mind that I switch my first focus to food as an example of how we judge.

My university students went through a phase of all wanting to do 'healthy eating' for their independent research projects. This was fine-ish, but usually amounted to no more than them policing (and criticising) what parents put in their children's lunchboxes. In no way did this sit comfortably with me. When my boys went through phases when all they had for lunch for weeks on end was jam sandwiches, it was not because I was lazy, or a bad parent, it was because anything else that I gave them came home uneaten. So a jam sandwich (on white bread) was better than nothing. It wasn't an indication that we had tea from the chippy every night, either – we actually ate reasonably healthily at home, which is why I knew a jam sandwich wasn't going to kill them. But again, it's back to those "white, middle-class norms of child rearing" (MacNaughton, 2003, p.261) that tell us that hummus and carrot sticks are *right* and a ham sandwich on white bread is an abomination. But there are even sub-strata to this snobbery. Johanna shared how the parents that sent their child to school with a lunch of avocado, matured cheese, and pancetta (see, not a nasty carb in sight) were still viewed as *getting it wrong*. As were the ones that gave their children whole chilis to munch on (because they liked them, not as some form of torture)…although I think I might agree with that one. These parents were not conforming to the general consensus of what a healthy lunch (as a typical white middle-class family) should look like.

We've a society which is still dominated by white British tradition despite the ethnic and cultural diversity of those living in it. Little by little we have decided that certain foods from other cultures are 'acceptable', they are adopted and anglicised until they bear little resemblance to the original dish (chicken madras and chili con carne being the obvious examples that spring to mind, wraps and flatbreads are also an acceptable, trendy alternative to breads these days). But we remain wary and dismissive of foods that stray from our *norm*. Especially those that are a bit more stinky than our delicate British noses are used to. In educational environments we are prone to buying into what we see as *acceptable* and *unacceptable* behaviours of parents, that help us to easily categorise them into those that are getting parenting right and those that are failing miserably. We need to remember that each family has its own culture where food is concerned. And that this will be influenced by family tradition, culture, and religion. There is no right or wrong here, hopefully just variety and colour (or not so much if you consider a cheese sandwich made with white bread). There may also be really sound reasons for that child always coming to school with sliced ham in white bread. Let's avoid judging lunchboxes, and let's also remember that unhealthy foods are far cheaper and far more readily available to those who are living in poverty.

I taught one very troubled boy whose parents were alcoholics and both extremely ill, and, therefore, not able to look after him properly. He took great delight in running off and hiding on top of or underneath things numerous times during the school day (oh, what fun we had getting him down from the top of high cupboards). To fuel his energy for this he inevitably arrived at school with handfuls of sticky sweets and alarming looking drinks in plastic containers with stabby straws (remember those? You know, the ones that are all plastic flavour?). His day was fuelled by enough refined sugars and artificial colours to give a healthy-sized whale the tremors. Presumably this is what he purchased with any lunch money he was given. I'm pretty sure that his parents, inebriated or not, did not bid him farewell in the morning with an instruction to buy the most sugar-laden, nutrient-devoid foods that he possibly

> could at the corner shop. His parents were not able to help him in the nurturing way that we expect of parents, they were suffering themselves. The very thought of us *telling them off* with a stern letter home is ridiculous. Instead, we did what we, as a setting could do to help. He was one of the children who was allowed to help himself to two school dinners every lunch time, and to hoover up as much milk and fruit as was available when his classmates had had their share.

Just to finish the *lunch box* focus, I had another student, a manager at a nursery, who told me that she wanted to look at healthy eating for her research project. My heart sank. She then explained that as several of her children spent long days at the nursery, she realised that she was providing them most of their nutrients for the day. She wanted to make sure that the diet that *she* provided was healthy enough. Now that's more like it. As educators let's focus upon what *we can do* to have a positive impact upon the wellbeing of the child, rather than making judgements about what others are not doing.

> I remember a colleague saying she bought fruit with her own money for children who often went without breakfast (for whatever reason – most were vulnerable children). She would quietly make this available for children in the morning with no fuss, no bother, no judgement.
>
> *Johanna*

What will always stay with me from the maintained nursery school research (Solvason, Webb, and Tsang, 2020), and the incredible individuals that were working there, was the total lack of judgement that was demonstrated toward parents, and the practitioners' seemingly boundless capacity to care. Much can be learned from their capacity to identify *problems* rather than *problem people* and to turn challenges into positive action. All of this was based upon the premise, as was outlined in the introduction, that they were on *the same team* and that whatever decisions were reached, it was unwaveringly about *keeping the child in mind*. The staff at these settings often mentioned Maslow's (1943) hierarchy of needs as their justification.

The nursery practitioners reasoned that the children had no hope of reaching their potential unless their basic needs of food, water, and safety were met, so that was their top priority. They raised funds to feed the children, they checked where the child had been sleeping, they gave information about mental health support, housing support, they gave free childcare to those who most needed it. You may be dubious about how any of this related to education, well, their principle was that unhappy children are not in a position to learn, and that happy parents equalled happy children. And the proof of the pudding, as they say, appeared to be in the eating. As I mentioned in the previous chapter, the development that the children demonstrated within their short time at these nurseries was phenomenal. If you ever get a chance, please do look at our full report for the amazing work that these settings are doing.

Most of my teaching took place in what would be considered as areas of deprivation. Unemployment, alcoholism, and drug addiction were all common within the families. A five-year-old commenting 'that looks like a block of hash' whilst modelling brown plasticene is just one of the many colourful memories that I have of the first school that I taught in. Many of the young girls aspired to be single mums as young as possible in order to get their own council flat. But I digress.

Somewhat ironically, one parent with quite extreme addiction problems was a taxi driver (let's hope her customers had good health insurance). She was extremely late to collect her children at least once a week and would often arrive under the influence. She worked at night, and as a result her children were looked after by a series of 'uncles' who seemed unaware of the concept of children needing sleep. I taught two of her children, and both would almost inevitably arrive at school late and exhausted. I remember them distinctly although it was nearly 20 years ago. The little girl, without fail, would come straight to me and crawl onto my lap for a cuddle. It didn't matter that she was nine years old, or that she had some of the biggest headlice I have seen in my entire life, she needed that cuddle. Both of these children, within minutes of arriving in the classroom, would make a beeline for the reading corner and the comfy cushions there. They would usually sleep until lunch. And yes, they also used to have two lunches. Attempting to educate these children had to take a back seat to their wellbeing.

APPROPRIATE ENGAGEMENT WITH PARENTS

As Lawson (2003) explains, understanding the parameters of parents' caring responsibilities and paid work is really important, because it is how these different life domains interact with the setting context which will impact on parents' engagement with the setting. We, as educators, tend to expect parents to have suitable jobs (i.e., respectable ones, or at least legal) that will enable them to provide for their children, at the same time as them being available within the working day for us to interact with them. This is based upon that good old, antiquated notion of the bread-winning father and the mother as domestic goddess (Lewis and West, 2016). Basically, when it comes to employment most parents are damned if they do and damned if they don't as far as settings are concerned. When are we going to realise that this picture of the stay-at-home mother no longer fits? In fact, let's face it, it doesn't fit most of the staff, never mind the parents.

As a parent, every parents' evening, school production, and class assembly that I attended reminded me of my *outsider* status as a working mum. There was the exclusive and high profile stay-at-home brigade (mainly mums), ready to jump to attention should a school trip need extra bodies, or costumes need fixing for the school play;

and then there were the rest of us. We were, quite frankly, a disappointment. We were conspicuous in our discomfort at parents' evenings (not just due to the tiny chairs that we couldn't fit on), having fled work with pressing tasks unfinished, for the pleasure of having our child's inadequacies presented to us in front of an audience. And, of course, if you didn't attend this humiliating theatre, then you were labelled as one of those parents that did not care; because no paid employment allows a parent to neglect their child in such a heartless way. I often wonder whether those many educators who are also parents have ever stopped to question this approach which borders on the barbaric, or at the very least, the inhumane? Why do schools do it?

The fact is that as flawed human beings we are all going to have our days of feeling inadequate. There are bound to be days when Earth Mother looks at Working Mother with awe, wishing that she, too, could juggle a career and parenting so 'effortlessly'. As parents we all become Oscar-worthy performers: we pretend it *doesn't matter* when our child has wet the bed for the third night in a row; we can be *super excited* at watching the same episode of Peppa Pig for the umpteenth time and we can enthusiastically usher our children to get ready in the morning when we are dying from exhaustion. Remember these things and try very hard to see the vulnerable *person* behind the stoic *parent* façade in your relationships with them.

REFLECTION POINT

Think about the last time that you invited parents into the setting. What was the reason for this and the format of this?

Try to imagine the encounter from the parents' perspective. What did you do to help those parents to feel welcome and comfortable? Was it a dialogue or a transmission of information?

In their US-based article, Chappel and Ratcliffe (2021) refer to Christenson and Sheridan's 2001 research, which "noted the importance of formal and informal communications" for building trusting relationships. This was absolutely the case in the nurseries that I researched with, in their 'why don't we go and get a cup of tea' when parents were distressed. Yet, as a parent, informal 'chats' with the teachers at my sons' schools were non-existent. I never experienced any sort of care, kindness, or concern for my sons' wellbeing outside of the setting, just demands. It was always about what the school required from me, what I should be doing that I wasn't.

Anderson and Minkle (2007) found in their survey of urban elementary school parents, that specific, personal invitations from teachers were far more influential on parent involvement than parents' sense of efficacy, the role that the school constructed for them or the resources available. Similarly, Chappel and Ratcliffe (2021) used their research results to argue that communication with parents needed to be personalised, that we need to remember that it is not about processes, because parents are individuals. They add that building a rapport with parents over the small stuff, means that you can "build rapport and establish trust before a high stakes event occurs" (Chappel and Ratcliffe, 2021, p.23). This was absolutely my experience with the parents of one of my most troublesome terrors (sorry, I mean darling pupils). I got to know the family of this particular seven-year-old boy, and their interests, really well. His mum and I probably chatted once or twice a week at picking up time about his behaviour in general and what he had been doing at home. This meant that on the times that I needed to tell mum that he had been an absolute little (… insert whatever word springs to mind) that day, I could do so with absolute frankness and honesty. Because she knew that I genuinely cared about the child, and that I, just like she and her partner, wanted what was best for him. Those little chats grew trust which enabled us to be on the same team.

REFLECTION POINT

How do you demonstrate genuine interest and care in the families that you work with?

'HARD-TO-REACH' PARENTS

If we find parents 'hard to reach' it is important to stop and ask ourselves 'why'? To be curious and ask yourself 'what else could be going on here?' During my divorce, in particular, I would most certainly have been considered 'hard to reach'. I was not at the school gates; I was not writing in reading records. Did that mean I didn't care? Of course not, I cared so much that it hurt. What it meant was that I couldn't, at that time, subscribe to the very narrowly set parameters for interaction that the school had set for us as parents; a set of expectations based upon the now largely defunct 'housewife'. If these expectations were beyond me, as an educated teacher with insider understanding of the education system, then just how achievable are they for others without the privilege of a similar education? Someone from another culture or someone with learning difficulties? I know, from the many passive aggressive messages that I received from my sons' primary school that I was perceived as *lazy*, that I just *couldn't be bothered*; these educators were blissfully unaware that with travel included my working day often stretched to 13 hours. And there will be many parents, in entirely different circumstances, whose day is just as demanding. But the impression that I had of my sons' educators, the way things looked from my perspective, was that they wouldn't have cared one jot if they had been aware; their only real concern was that I was not playing by the rules of the game that they had created, the one with the goal of getting them further up the school league tables.

As I have already mentioned, Lawson (2003) explains how understanding the details of parents' caregiving and paid work, as well as their role at school, is vital, because it is how the domains of work, family, and school interact that will determine the shape of the parent partnership created. And it is these types of informal chats, however brief, that enable parents to feel "connected" to the setting (Chappel and Ratliffe, 2021). At times like this, as educators, we become armed with the necessary information to be able to consider more effectively, 'what is best for this child in this situation?' If any of my boys' teachers had dedicated the same amount of time taken to scribing reprimanding comments in a reading record, to asking whether there was any reason I was not reading with my son at home, then they would have understood the situation. And then I'm sure that any number of the volunteers that were always found at the school could have heard my son read, and even written in his reading record ... but they never did.

An example of this genuine regard and consideration for an individual's situation was clear in a conversation that I had with a nursery school leader about a parent who was struggling. This single parent had two children with special needs and a third with behavioural issues. Because of the child's behaviour issues he was expelled from several nurseries. She had hoped that this nursery might take him.

Despite the situation this woman was not viewed by the nursery as a problem, or a failed parent, rather she was viewed as someone who was doing her best and was struggling. She was currently working, and her child being expelled from the latest setting meant that she was in danger of losing her job to stay at home to care for him. This leader recognised that this might be the challenge that would 'tumble her house of cards'. Regardless of a limited capacity, the nursery took on the child and assured the mother that he would not be a problem with them. The leader finished recounting this story to me with 'and he's doing great'.

BUILDING RELATIONSHIPS ACROSS DIVIDES (CAREFULLY)

I hope that these examples encourage you, no matter how busy or stressed you are, to try to "inhabit the other person's castle" as Somekh (1994) puts it, and find out why there might be an issue or a challenge communicating with certain parents, to try to understand why the fortress might seem impenetrable. A more direct approach may not be the way forward with some parents, sometimes trust can be slow to grow. One MNS leader had a large wall map in her reception area, which she used as a prompt for discussion of cultural heritage. This acted as a non-threatening way of opening the door to communication, of showing interest and curiosity. Do not forget that "trust is built in the quiet moments and these moments are not to be underestimated" (Riley, 2017, p.19).

REFLECTION POINT

Think about parents who you have worked with that you might traditionally have considered 'hard to reach'. Ask yourself:

1. What was the issue? Why did I consider them hard to reach?
2. What did I know about what was going on for that family in that moment?
3. What else might have been causing some issues?
4. What else might I have needed to be aware of?
5. What else could I have done to support them?

Consider carefully what you do well and what you might like to change.

CONCLUSION

Ensuring that every voice, however different, is heard, is harder than it might appear. It does, as pointed out by Olsson (2009), require us to be comfortable with the potentially uncomfortable and to give up our sense of control within the educator–parent dynamic. If we are honest, we know as educators that we like to feel in control. I still have recurring nightmares of being in a teaching situation where I don't, where I am being ignored, and chaos is setting in. I wish I were joking. But we also want to regain control because we are aware of performance and outcomes-driven demands (Hayes and Filipovic, 2018, p.221; Basford, 2019). What we rarely consider is that parents are doing exactly the same, they want to feel in some sort of control, too. They want to ensure that their child is going to be okay. It can feel uncomfortable when our sense of control is threatened or taken away, because we are allowing others to influence our success or failure. But it is important to remember that at the very core of education are relationships; as Jarvis (1995, p.25) puts it, "the ethic of concern for persons ... forms the very essence of education itself". And concern means respecting, and listening to. Let's not forget this in our quest for more measurable results.

Whilst we might argue that as educators our espoused theory is child-centric (in line with current trends in pedagogic thinking), we can forget the value of applying the same thinking to the families that we work with. Is our practice family-centric? What do we do to ensure that our families feel respected and trusted that they have their child's best interests at heart? How do we make them feel, regardless of their cultural heritage, education, or socio-economic status, that they are part of a proactive, trusting, and sustainable relationship (Prowle and Hodgkins 2020, p.13)? Well, just like any other relationship, this needs to be built upon dialogue. Only through dialogue can you come to understand "children's participation within their families' and communities' activities" and only then can "children experience a continuity of understandings and expectations between home and education settings which, in turn, can foster their enthusiasm for learning" (Chan and Ritchie, 2016, p.291). As the leaders in nurseries stressed when discussing their relationships with parents, it's not about us, it's not about them, it is about what is best for the child. How can we build relationships, *especially* with those parents who are struggling, or those parents who are absent, for the best outcomes for the child?

In order to meet the needs of the diverse families in our care we simply need to talk far less and listen far more. Roberts (2017, p.8) discusses the use of "reflective listening", hearing parents (and children) in a "non-judgemental" and "non-threatening" way. Always start from that position of unconditional positive regard; let the only presumption that you have about parents be that they want what is best for the child. If behaviours seem to suggest otherwise, well, then do your best to find out why that may be – never simply assume a lack of care. I'll finish this chapter with my favourite-ever quote from my favourite-ever theorist, about what we think we know:

> Be aware … that things will continue to change; this includes your knowledge claim. You should always hold your knowledge lightly, and be aware that what you know today may change tomorrow. Always remember that you may, after all, be mistaken.
>
> McNiff, 2010, p.106

KEY POINTS TO TAKE AWAY FROM THIS CHAPTER

1. Avoid making judgements built upon first impressions; take time to get to know parents as individuals.
2. The 'nuclear family' is a totally outdated model; consider whether you are still advocating this.
3. Instead of making judgements of parents based upon things like a "white middle-class" view of what a lunchbox should contain, focus upon what you can do in the setting to support children who seem not to be getting all that they need. Do the children always have access to fresh fruit, fresh drinking water? Is there a space for them to rest, spare clothes for them to wear?
4. Understand that *one size doesn't fit all* when it comes to communication and consider alternative means. When at all possible, make that communication personalised.
5. Always start from a position of unconditional positive regard for parents, just as you would hope they would do for you.

TEAM ACTIVITY

Considering Different Lenses

How welcoming might your setting appear through the eyes of the different (non-traditional) families in your community?

Consider specific family groups (use the examples below or any others that you are aware of).

- Families who may have experienced/be experiencing divorce or separation.
- Families who might have gone through/be going through adoption or fostering.
- Families of differing race, religion, or culture.
- Non-English-speaking families.
- Grandparents as carers.
- Much younger and much older parents.
- Stay-at-home mothers and fathers.
- Parents who work long hours.
- Same sex and LGBTQ families and families who might be non-binary or gender neutral.
- Families from differing socio-economic statuses.
- Families with SEND requirements.

In what ways do you:

1. Ensure they feel welcomed and accepted?
2. Endeavour to open/sustain a dialogue with them?
3. Show them that you value their perspective?
4. Show them that you understand their specific struggles?
5. Show flexibility to work around their needs?

REFERENCES

Anderson, K. and Minkle, K. (2007). Parent involvement in education: toward an understanding of parents' decision making. *Journal of Educational Research*, 100, 311–323.

Basford, J. (2019). Being a graduate professional in the field of early childhood education and care: silence, submission and subversion. *Education 3-13*, 47(7), 862–875.

Brooker, L. (2010). Constructing the triangle of care: power and professionalism in practitioner/parent relationships. *British Journal of Educational Studies*, 58(2), 181–196.

Chan, A. and Ritchie, J. (2016). Parents, participation, partnership: problematising New Zealand early childhood education. *Contemporary Issues in Early Childhood*, 17(3), 289–303.

Chappel, J. and Ratliffe, K. (2021). Factors impacting positive school–home communication: a multiple case study of family–school partnership practices in eight elementary schools in Hawai'i. *School Community Journal*, 31(2), 9–30.

Cliffe, J. and Solvason, C. (2019). Should we consider rhizomatic thinking when educating young minds? *NZ International Research in Early Childhood Education Journal*, 22(1), 86–100.

Cliffe, J. and Solvason, C. (2020). The role of emotions in building new knowledge and developing young children's understanding. *Power and Education*, 12(2), 189–203. https://doi.org/10.1177/1757743820930724.

Cooper, C. (2009). Parent involvement, African American mothers, and the politics of educational care. *Equity & Excellence in Education*, 42, 379–394.

Haines Lyon, C. (2018). Democratic parent engagement: relational and dissensual. *Power and Education*, 10(2), 195–208.

Hayes, N. and Filipović, K. (2018). Nurturing 'buds of development': from outcomes to opportunities in early childhood practice. *International Journal of Early Years Education*, 26(3), 220–232.

Jarvis, P. (1995). Teachers and learners in adult education: transaction or moral interaction? *Studies in the Education of Adults*, 27(1), 24–36.

Lawson, M.A. (2003). School-family relations in context: parent and teacher perceptions of parent involvement. *Urban Education*, 38, 77–133.

Lewis, J. and West, A. (2016). Early childhood education and care in England under austerity: continuity or change in political ideas, policy goals, availability, affordability and quality in a childcare market? *Journal of Social Policy*. http://eprints.lse.ac.uk/67492/.

MacNaughton, G. (2003). *Shaping early childhood: learners, curriculum and contexts*. Maidenhead: Open University Press.

Maslow, A.H. (1943). A theory of human motivation. *Psychological Review*, 50, 370–396.

McNiff, J. (2010). *Action research for professional development*. Dorset: September Books.

Moll, L.C. and Greenberg, J. (1990). Creating zones of possibilities: combining social contexts for instruction. In L. C. Moll (ed.), *Vygotsky and education*. Cambridge: Cambridge University Press, 319–348.

Olsson, L. (2009). *Movement and experimentation in young children's learning: Deleuze and Guattari in early childhood education*. Oxon: Routledge.

Oostdam, R. and Hooge, E. (2013). Making the difference with active parenting; forming educational partnerships between parents and schools. *European Journal of the Psychology of Education*, 28, 337–351.

Posey-Maddox, L. and Haley-Lock, A. (2020). One size does not fit all: understanding parent engagement in the contexts of work, family, and public schooling. *Urban Education*, 55(5), 671–698.

Prowle, A. and Hodgkins, A. (2020). *Making a difference with children and families re-imagining the role of the practitioner*. London: Red Globe Press.

Riley, K.A. (2017). *Place, belonging and school leadership: researching to make the difference*. London: Bloomsbury Academic.

Roberts, W. (2017). Trust, empathy and time: relationship building with families experiencing vulnerability and disadvantage in early childhood education and care services. *Australasian Journal of Early Childhood*, 42(4), 4–12.

Solvason, C., Webb, R. and Sutton-Tsang, S. (2020). Evidencing the effects of maintained nursery schools' roles in early years sector improvements. Available from: https://tactyc.org.uk/research/.

Somekh, B. (1994). Inhabiting each other's castles: towards knowledge and mutual growth through collaboration. *Educational Action Research*, 2(3), 357–381.

Wilson, T. (2016). *Working with parents, carers and families in the early years: the essential guide*. London: Routledge.

CHAPTER 3
Developing Trust

Johanna Cliffe

Bok (1978, cited in Baier, 1986, p.231) explains that "whatever matters to human beings, trust is the atmosphere in which it thrives" and few would dispute that trust is a key component of any relationship or partnership. If your partner does try and dispute it, then you are probably on rocky ground. Roberts (2017, p.5) goes so far as to suggest that trust is a concept that, alongside honesty, empathy, and respect, is a cornerstone of meaningful communication and authentic and respectful social interactions. Much of the literature that explores building relationships, positive communications, partnerships, and partnership working, mentions trust or trustworthiness in some form or another. Trust, it appears, is a quality that we, as individuals, and certainly as educators, hope to project in ourselves and also seek to find in others. Most of us are cut to the core if our trustworthiness is questioned. Yet the literature on this topic, like so much of the touchy-feely stuff, is extremely vague about exactly what trust is, why it is so important and just how it can be successfully fostered.

REFLECTION POINT

Before you read any further in this chapter, spend five minutes writing your own definition of trust. You do not have to share this with anyone, but it is important that this is your view, your initial thoughts before any further discussion of trust has been undertaken. Save this definition for later in the chapter.

In the plethora of documents which mention parent partnership working there is no shortage of reference to 'building trust' and

DOI: 10.4324/9781003191209-3

'trusting relationships'; you may also find vague reference to the length of time this will take to develop. What is less prevalent is discussion concerning just *how* practitoners can go about building these trusting relationships. There is an expectation that trust can, and will, be nurtured through positive co-parenting scenarios, with an assumption that practitoners 'just know' how to do this, as if merely telling us that this is important is all that is needed for it to magically happen. On the contrary, our own experience of working with educators, and especially those who are relatively new to the profession, suggests that some practitioners can be terrified to even speak to a parent, let alone feel confident in building a trusting relationship with them (something explored by Solvason, Hodgkins, and Watson, 2021). So clearly this is not quite as straightforward as the literature assumes.

Although literature, such as Wilson (2018, p.91), argues that there are no special skills or training required to build trusting relationships, I am a little more dubious. Knowing that it is considered best practice to cultivate trust and a trusting culture (and that without this parent partnership cannot hope to be successful) and understanding *how* to go about establishing trusting relationships, are very different undertakings. Working with families, particularly vulnerable families, to build trusting relationships, is tough, and many practitoners feel ill-equipped to even begin this kind of work (Roberts, 2017). Therefore, trust building, as with many of the other relational skills, becomes a seed that we, as educators, know that we need to plant, but often have no real notion how to nurture it. It is for these reasons that this chapter seeks to examine trust and trustworthiness in more detail, and to consider practical ways that we, as educators, can develop trust and trusting relationships within our practice.

REFLECTION POINT

Now let's think about the concept of trust in context.

Exercise 1

Think about someone you trust implicitly; why do you trust them? Note your thoughts about what it is they specifically do or say that makes them a trusted person for you.

Consider what it is about their behaviour towards you; their actions as well as their words, that makes them a person you trust.

Exercise 2

Think about someone you do not trust and repeat the exercise.

Consider what conclusions you can draw about the concept of trust? Are there any qualities or actions that you feel are more important regarding either trust or distrust? Why?

Keep these notes to refer to later.

While the above exercise may seem simple, it does provide a window into trust and the potential features of trustworthiness. Until any of us understand the concept of trust, considering how it can be nurtured in our professional relationships remains a pretty vacuous, intellectual exercise.

STARTING AT THE BEGINNING … THE TRIANGLE OF TRUST

If I were to suggest that you give your car to a stranger to look after I imagine you would refuse. If I told you to withdraw all of your money from the bank and ask a stranger to take care of it for you, again, you would probably laugh and at the ridiculousness of the suggestion and refuse. So, compare these examples to the response if I were to suggest to a parent that they allow a total stranger to take care of something as precious as their child. Yet within our culture we do this all the time. Garages are entrusted with cars, banks and building societies with our money and, yes, practitoners with children. Trustworthiness is viewed as an inherent characteristic of the educator.

Now I am sure there are those of you reading this that will say but educators are *known*, they are key figures in the community, or at the very least you will have friends or family with experience of said individual. However, for many of us this is not the case. Even though I lived in tight-knit rural communities for most of my life, as a child I rarely set eyes on my educators before that first day of school. My parents could have been leading me to the lair of Mrs Trunchbull. Similarly, as a parent, my child's educators were strangers to me until my children landed in their class. And as an educator, whilst there were a few parents that I vaguely knew from my school days or as friends, mostly the sea of parents and children were new faces to me, year in and year out. So, during those early days of the new school year, despite the glut of transition activities we tick box our way through, just how much do parents and practitoners really know about each other? What is the trust that exists based upon?

Schweizer et al. (2017) suggest that in education trust has both implicit and explicit dimensions. Fundamentally, trust is intertwined with our implicit (those personal ideas, or values, that we have about how a person should behave, that we do not necessarily speak out loud) and explicit (the clear, visible rules recognised and discussed by all) expectations. If implicit understandings of trust are not shared then this can have negative implications for any partnership working and, ultimately, the outcomes for children and families. While it could be argued that in the initial stages of the educator–parent–child triadic relationship there is, regardless of each player's knowledge of one another, a level of trusting and entrusting present, Schweizer et al. (2017, p.101) remind us that the successful functioning of the relationship over time is what generates trust. It is a 'chicken and egg' scenario that has not been tackled in any of the teaching standards that I have come across. We are asking parents to blindly trust someone that they do not know, and understandably this can cause anxiety.

> Even 22 years later I still clearly remember the anxiety that I felt when I first left my baby with someone other than his dad. Would they know how to comfort him properly? Would they make sure that he had his blanket? What if he missed me too much? The only times I felt that I was properly fulfilling my duties as a mum when my first son was very small,

> were when he was in my arms, or at least in my gaze. My eldest son, as I am writing this, is working in Scotland and my youngest is studying in America. It does get easier to let them go and know that they will be safe, but it doesn't get easier to deal with any situation where you feel they are being treated unfairly. I've had to stop myself from giving my son's boss, or coach, an earful on many an occasion. The urge to protect your child really is overwhelming.
>
> *Carla*

Trust is something that we rarely verbalise (unless within the context of romantic relationships) therefore we need to be more aware of the presence of, and give more consideration to how we navigate, implicit trust. Fisher and Tallant (2020) explore how, from the parents' perspective, trust, trustworthiness, and reliance intermingle in a powerful way. Wilson (2018, p.93) discusses "the extreme act of faith" that parents perform, in order to feel comfortable leaving their children in a stranger's care. It is not like leaving the child with a known (and loved) relative, they do not *know* what their child's experience will be with this stranger. It makes no difference how much research parents conduct before choosing an educational provision for their children, their knowledge of the day-to-day experience for their child there will always be incomplete (Schweizer et al., 2017).

Although it might be assumed that educational provisions are entrusted to be vigilant in ensuring practitoners are DBS checked (i.e. not to be found on any offenders lists anywhere), have the right qualifications (Webster, 2018) and adhere to professional expectations (Fisher and Tallant, 2020), trustworthiness is about so much more than this. In truth, parents have no way to know exactly *how* you will interact with their children when they are in your care; therefore, the trust that parents place in us, as educators, requires that they make both themselves and their children vulnerable (Schweizer et al., 2017). And this position of vulnerability is one that no-one would place themselves in out of choice.

REFLECTION POINT

Return to the list you created at the beginning of this chapter. Can you identify:

- Implicit and explicit elements within the concept trust?
- What is obvious through action?
- What is inferred or implied?
- What is verbalised and what is simply felt?

Reflect upon what this might tell us about our own understanding of trust and trustworthiness and what this understanding is based upon.

Within this triadic, parent–educator–child relationship, it is also important to acknowledge the trust displayed by children. Some children skip happily into settings with ne'er a backward glance (to the relief of parents and practitoners alike), however, as we all know, there are those children who will become withdrawn, clingy, and distressed. For these children, each morning is more like a walk to the gallows than the opportunity to spend time with friends. I have lost count of the times, I have heard this being laid at the door of attachment theory; the child is insecurely attached, it's the parents' fault they didn't prepare them enough and are clearly *making it worse*. Equally, practitoners might be blamed for not being skilful enough in handling the situation, for not stepping in at the right time and taking charge. But it is important to be aware that what is actually happening in this situation is that the child is saying "my trust isn't there yet". And when you really stop and think about it, that is a perfectly reasonable reaction to a new and scary situation. Biesta (2013, p.44) suggests that children are often the ones with the power in an educative relationship as education is "an act of gift giving" and it is children who decide to "welcome the gift". Until children can trust us, as educators, to take them on that next step, learning cannot happen.

What is less well considered in many books about trust is the final dynamic within this triadic relationship, which is that as practitoners we need to have a level of implicit trust in parents, too. Hawley (2014) and Fisher and Tallant (2020) suggest that as educators, we trust parents to bring their children to our settings and rely on them to be willing to work with us. There is a tacit agreement or what Schweizer et al. (2017, p.100) refer to as an implicit social contract where practitoners trust parents to believe in their professional capacity to 'do their jobs'. It is important to recognise that while parents and practitoners might be encouraged to consider each other as experts in the child's needs, this is a complex dynamic (as, I'm sure, many of you are well aware). In practice, both parent and practitioner tend to look to each other for validation, at the same time as judging one other based upon the limited perspective of their own context and experience (Solvason, Cliffe, and Bailey, 2019).

A colleague, who was teaching in a primary school, came to the university to deliver a teaching session to my final-year students. During the session she mentioned behaviour charts – you know, those tools of humiliation that are placed on classroom walls to let the world know which children can conform perfectly and which are failures at it? Okay, from my comment there, you have probably guessed that this is not the type of approach that we encourage our students to take to managing (or, more appropriately, understanding) children's behaviour. But the reason that I mention it, is because as soon as the words "behaviour chart" left my colleague's lips, all of my students turned to look at me in mild horror. Within our cosy university context, and as a result of discussions on our course, my students' perspective was that this chart was something 'bad', yet within that school it was seen as a positive approach to behaviour management. Our views are, very much, influenced by our experience.

We must always recognise, as educators, that although we see something as 'right' others may have a different opinion, and they are perfectly entitled to that. Just remember the image of the little men looking at a symbol on the floor, stood facing one another, at opposite ends. One insists it's a 6 and one insists it's a 9. Neither is right or wrong, they simply haven't tried looking from the other perspective yet.

The first day of this new partnership, everyone within the triad is in precisely the same space regarding their feelings about each other. As Cruz (2019, p.934) observes, "we typically want to know if they will be an ally or a threat, a source of security or of hazard, a collaborator or an adversary, honest or shifty". In essence, we are looking to see who we can trust and if our trust is well placed, therefore making someone trustworthy, while contemplating how we ourselves are being seen and judged, weighed, and measured. Within this new moment there is an unspoken pause, or as Fisher and Tallant (2020, p.781) suggest, a place within practice where, theoretically speaking, neither trust nor mistrust (or active distrust) exists yet within the relationship. This is both a powerful and a scary place. The potential within the new collaboration is, at that moment, without bounds. However, this potential is often tempered by the previous educational experiences (whether as learner, parent, or educator) and societal preconceptions that we bring to the encounter. Positive experiences will breed positive expectations and, unfortunately, vice versa.

To complicate this already complex social situation still further, there is the additional fact that trust is extremely personal. Tschannen-Moran (2014, p.19) notes that judgements and priorities are personally and contextually bound, key requirements for dispensing levels of trust will vary significantly between individuals. If you were to complete the initial reflective activity, where you defined trust, now, would your definition remain the same? And what are the chances that your definition was precisely the same as someone else's? Slim, I would argue. Most literature functions from the assumption that trust is a concept that is universally understood and defined, however, this is not case. Our perception of this abstract concept, like so many personal characteristics, is entirely personal, and fluid.

REFLECTION POINT

This section of the chapter has briefly considered the role of expectations and *knowing* that impact on the educator–parent–child

---

relationship. Awareness and sensitivity are key at this early stage for supporting and navigating these early and unknown waters.

Consider the following questions and make notes on any responses you feel are relevant:

1. What do you *know* about each parent and child when they first attend?
2. What do they *know* about you?
3. What expectations do you and your setting have of parents on that first day of working together?
4. What expectations do you have of the children who are new to your provision/class?
5. What expectations do you suppose parents have of you?

Review these notes and consider your initial list of qualities that inspire trust and distrust. What connections can you see? Do you identify areas for development?

DEFINITIONS OF TRUST

As previously stated, the concept of trust is one that is often assumed to be universally known and understood, yet returning to your initial definition, how easy did you find it to write? It seems sensible, before discussing further ways of fostering trusting relationships within our practice, to give some time to developing a shared understanding of what, exactly, trust is.

Fisher and Tallant (2020, p.782) argue that our language is somewhat "fast and loose" when we express an expectation of concepts such as trust, whereas often there is no agreed understanding of exactly what it means in practice. Nebulous phrases such as "multifaceted phenomena" (Curtis, 2011, p.54) or "invisible social glue" (Cruz, 2019, p.934) are offered by some authors, while others simply discuss its importance without actually attempting to define it at all. Baier (1994, p.98) once boldly claimed that "trust is a phenomenon we are so familiar with we scarcely notice its presence and variety". And because of this, we rarely question it. That being said, it would appear that those sources that do define it, see trust as something that bridges vulnerability and risk. Baier (1994, p.1050) simplistically suggests that "trust is letting other persons take care of something the truster cares about, where such 'caring for' involves some exercise of discretionary power". Rousseau et al. (1998) cited in Campagne et al. (2020, p.995) describe trust as "a psychological state comprising the intention to accept vulnerability based upon positive expectations of the intentions or behaviour of another". And Curtis (2011, p.54) explains that trust "involves elements of risk and vulnerability on the behalf of the trusting individual" and is a prerequisite for collaborative, interpersonal (relational) partnership working. But there are still more definitions: Hawley (2014, p.10) argues that "to trust someone to do something is to believe that she has a commitment to doing it, and to rely upon her to meet that commitment". Whereas Tschannen-Moran (2014, p.19) defines trust as "a willingness to be vulnerable to another based on the confidence that the other is benevolent, honest, open, reliable, and competent". And, needless to say, if I kept searching, I could find many, many, more interpretations. Which most resonates with you?

So, while many definitions of trust do have similarities, or key themes, these existing definitions do remain rather less concrete than is useful. What may be helpful, then, is to consider some key components that we, as educators, could identify to develop a shared understanding (and to identify ways forward). For example, Hawley (2014, p.1) suggests that whilst definitions remain somewhat unsatisfactory, two assumptions can be made, and these are that: trust involves "two people and a task" and that "trust involves expectations about both competence and willingness". Of course, trust can (and frequently does) involve more than two people, however, the uncomplicated notion that it depends upon individuals and a task may be helpful for us moving forward. Therefore, if we accept that trust is relational and involves a task, but also (perhaps more importantly) that it pertains to being vulnerable and taking a risk, this may be a good place to start. But the question remains, how do we actually foster it?

Tschannen-Moran's (2014, p.39) definition contained what she considered five facets of trust, which are also useful in considering the development of it. These are:

1. Benevolence which demonstrates goodwill and caring.
2. Honesty which relates to a level of perceived integrity and authenticity.
3. Openness demonstrated by a willingness to be vulnerable and share experiences and communicate.
4. Reliability and consistency within interactions.
5. Competence relating to skills, knowledge, and ability.

Considering how we employ the five facets within our practice might provide a useful foundation for developing and maintaining trusting relationships within our practice.

REFLECTION POINT

Consider each of the five components of trust mentioned above. List what you do within your practice that might develop each aspect in relation to the educator–parent–child relationship and your daily provision. What do you do well? What needs improvement?

If it helps, you could colour-code your responses using a traffic light method. Things you feel you do well in green, things you do but think could still be improved in amber, and finally anything that does not work or that you could do but for whatever reason do not as red. This can be used as a self, or provision audit for development.

A final note about vulnerability, particularly in light of Tscahnnen-Moran's third point: as practitoners it is important to remember that whilst we do not like feeling vulnerable, (any more than a parent does), vulnerability can be an antecedent to trust. As practitoners we want to exude control and competence, and showing vulnerability does not align with this image. Yet when one person demonstrates vulnerability to another, a personal risk is accepted in the implicit mutual agreement that trust will not be violated (Hallam et al., 2014, p.146). Over time the interactions that this inspires can generate deep and lasting feelings of trust. When Carla did some research with cluster groups of primary and special school head teachers, what was mentioned again and again throughout conversations was the trust that had developed between these leaders and how it provided a 'safety-net' for them as professionals. What is interesting here, though, is that they also all stressed that there needed to be an element of vulnerability, of showing that you were not perfect, for trust to develop. A key action in doing this was that the leaders visited one another's schools on a normal working day and saw it 'warts and all', its strengths and its weaknesses. This then gave a starting point from which to discuss ideas of development (see Solvason and Kington, 2019, for more about this research). If we are to form trusting relationships with parents, we, likewise, must be willing to show that we are not perfect, that we do not have all the answers, and that we are open to ideas of development and improvement.

EXPECTATIONS AND HIERARCHY

When there is a good balance within the educator–parent–child relationship, our role encompasses elements of support, effective signposting for early intervention, and the reciprocal sharing of ideas and strategies. This nurtures trust through positive co-parenting scenarios, which can improve outcomes for the children and families in our care. However, when working with parents it is really important that our espoused beliefs, our values that we hold about working in partnership with parents, and the reality of what we actually do, align closely. No one trusts an individual who is 'all talk'.

Tschannen-Moran (2014, p.54) notes that trust is built strongly where there is common ground regarding values and attitudes. This is reminiscent of Somehk (1994, p.365) who suggested that true collaboration requires understanding which can only come with knowing what it is like to be in the others' shoes, or "inhabiting each other's castles". Issues can arise when perceptions or realities do not align due to value-based, moral, and cultural disparities (Fisher and Tallant, 2020, p.781), therefore it is vital to focus upon where your values do overlap. As one early years' leader reported in Solvason, Webb, and Sutton-Tsang (2020, p.53), the way to meet cultural disparities is to actively seek common ground in terms of the wellbeing of the child, "Because … it doesn't matter that half of our children have languages that the staff don't speak. We can still engage really well together because we've got a common purpose".

Goodall (2018, p.604) argues that while educational provision has shifted strongly towards learner-centric teaching, partnership with parents and attitudes to parental involvement have for many settings remained stuck in transmission approaches. In other words, educationalists instruct, and parents listen. Friere's (1994, p.106) description of this approach is that we, as educationalists, hold knowledge that needs to be "deposited" or transferred, in this case to parents, in an authoritarian manner. Within this scenario parents cannot possibly feel trusted or respected by educationalists. It is not that parents' contributions are not valued; they are not even invited to make them. At the risk of sounding like a stuck record, it is important that as educationalists we find space to listen and demonstrate to parents that their own views on their child's education are valid, even on those occasions when they do not align with our own.

The impact that expectations can have upon trust is particularly well articulated in Choi's (2017) account of education provision in America. She shared how her feelings of excitement and anticipation as a parent soon deteriorated into disillusionment, disappointment, and disempowerment when her son entered the education system there. Instead of the shared partnership she had hoped for, practitoners were only concerned with compliance, and this is exactly what they sought from her. This is not an isolated incident; in our previous work we shared our own experiences, as parents, of interactions with teachers which were neither an informative dialogue nor a respectful and sensitive conversation (Solvason, Cliffe, and Bailey, 2019, p.193) they were instructions, or worse, beratements. I probably don't need to mention again here the critical monologues or passive aggressive reading record comments that many of us, as parents, have received (but I will). How many of us, as parents, have asked the same questions as Choi (2017, p.49), who wondered whether teachers even "care who I am, how I raise my son, what my struggles are as a parent". While Choi is South Korean, and her concerns were specific to how her cultural values and heritage were to be respected, issues around trust and parental exclusion are by no means limited to cultural heritage. Judgements made about social status, wealth, educational experience, even physical appearance can all impact upon the development of successful working relationships.

Riley (2017, p.4) discusses how belonging is an innate human need and that within education we have a "crisis of belonging". We all need to trust that education is a safe space no matter whether we are an educator, parent, or child. However, it is reasonable to argue that the responsibility for creating safe spaces and a feeling of belonging is very much in the hands of the educator. For example, an 'open-door' policy is something that regarded as 'good' and inclusive practice where parents are concerned. The idea that the door is always open for parents to walk though and that practitioners are always available when needed, seems on the surface like something to strive for. However, if we consider vulnerability, who is taken out of their comfort zone here? At first glance it may seem like the educator, put openly on display, yet for a dialogue to take place, the parent is required to step into the educators' domain. The limitations of this approach are highlighted in the research of Solvason, Webb, and Sutton-Tsang (2020) where one nursery leader explained: "I won't say we have an open door … I will go out there, do you see what I mean? And if somebody isn't coming in, I will go out into the car park" (ibid, p.53). For parent partnerships to thrive within a traditionally hierarchical context, sometimes practitioners need to make that first move. They have to make themselves vulnerable and step out of their own secure school fortress to meet the parent; whether this is metaphorically or literally will depend on the parent and the circumstances. Essentially, we need to work on ways to ensure that parents and their children feel they belong, and that we co-exist in a non-judgemental community.

REFLECTION POINT

The questions below consider Goodall's (2018, p.611) way to reimagine the banking model, the idea that learning is "deposited" or "transferred" onto parents.

Use the questions to reflect on your own practice, try to be specific and think of the actual strategies that you use; what do you say and do?

1. How do you enable parents to participate in supporting the learning of their child?
2. How do you show parents that you value the knowledge that they bring to the partnership?
3. What systems do you have in place to support practitoner and parent dialogue?
4. Do practitoners and parents within your setting respect the legitimate authority of each other's roles and contributions to supporting learning? How do you know?

Having reflected on these questions, consider your list about trust that you made at the very beginning of this chapter and your additions from the five facets of trust. How might your answers to the above reflective questions begin to build trusting relationships? What do you do well? What changes might you need to make?

THE IMPACT OF ACCOUNTABILITY CULTURE

Feelings of disillusionment, lack of value, and isolation do not only apply to parents, practitoners can also experience these. The increased accountability and process-driven marketisation that we now see in the education system, with parents sitting firmly in the position of consumer, also places us, as educators, in a diminished situation. As our pedagogical approaches are increasingly prescribed and monitored and we become less able to enact our professional roles with any level of autonomy or freedom (Schweizer et al., 2017), we can often feel that our own decisions are not trusted. The challenge is how, within this context, we create trusting relationships where we can all feel equally listened to and respected. Where no individual, whether educator, parent, nor child is silenced, and where the 'good' parent and 'good' educator are not synonymous with mere conformity.

The accountability of a marketised system of education, has been accused of operating in a way that causes practitoners to refrain from placing trust in students (or parents) within the learning process (Rogers, 1951, p.427). After all, it is the practitoner that will 'pay the price' of poor attainment, in some cases literally, in schools that implement results-driven salary systems. However, a truly person-centred focus to educator–parent–child relationships and interactions, as defined by Rogers (1951), would require that we operate as if that trust is already present, it is a given. Rogers' belief is that by unequivocally treating all players as trustworthy this will change the way that we approach interactions. That how we behave, and our actions from the outset, will naturally promote more trust-filled and meaningful encounters and experiences.

CONCLUSION

Moving forward we need to consider how we are promoting the five key facets of trust, as defined by Tschannen-Moran (2014, p.39): benevolence, honesty, openness, reliability, and competence, within our practice. What does this 'look like' in your settings? What, specifically, do you say and do? If "trust is built in quiet moments" (Riley, 2017, p.19), are you using these moments wisely? Perhaps this is something that you could consider as a team, or even as a whole school.

Our communications with families need to be person and family centred (Rogers, 1951) and jargon free. We need to practice reflective listening and making sure we are ready to hear and act on parents' views and contributions. When issues arise, ask yourself 'what else could be going on here?' Be curious, ask questions rather than giving commands, do this to shift your thinking and, as a result, your actions and reactions. It is within these moments of genuine dialogue and the resulting actions that trustworthiness can be nurtured. We need to remember, as educators, that while it may not always feel entirely comfortable, we sometimes need to be the first to be vulnerable and to reach out, to celebrate and share with parents, to walk out into the car park. It is important to remember that when it comes to educating our children, we really are all in this together.

KEY POINTS TO TAKE AWAY FROM THIS CHAPTER

1. Trust is a key facet of any relationship or partnership.
2. Parents demonstrate a considerable amount of trust in us, as educators, by leaving their precious children with us; that makes them vulnerable.
3. We should be willing to step outside of our comfort zone and become vulnerable, too, to enable trust to develop.
4. The importance of finding 'common ground' with parents regarding values and attitudes.
5. Not to allow the pressures and demands of a marketised education system prevent trust from forming.

TEAM ACTIVITY

Developing Trust

The purpose of this chapter was to explore trust and trustworthiness in more detail in order to consider practical ways in which we, as educators, can develop trust and trusting relationships within our practices. Essentially, there are no quick fixes or easy answers, it is about working towards feelings of trust and understanding what makes us and parents feel trusted and trustworthy.

In their book, *Beyond the Bake Sale*, Henderson et al. (2007, p.14) note that there are several perspectives that settings take that can either help or hinder partnership working and levels of trust. In their account of partnership working, Pugh and De'Ath (1989) consider the agency of parents within different styles of partnership. It can be useful to explore where your setting fits within these parameters and how this might foster partnership working. It might be, for example, that you feel the majority of your parents 'fit' into the category of non-participatory or supporter parents, but why is this?

Use the table below, influenced by Henderson et al. (2007, p.14) and Pugh and De'Ath (1989) and consider where you would place your setting and the parents you work with.

Message given by the setting	Make yourself at home The needs of the child are the focus with educators, parents and the community working together in full partnership.	Come on in Parents are welcome to be involved, partnership is under development.	We'll send an invite Parent involvement is welcomed, when required by the setting.	Not today thanks Parents are not invited in. School and home life should be kept separate.
View of parents	**Parents as partners** Parents fully involved and able to make decisions about implementation.	**Parents as participators** Parents as helpers and learners. Parents participate in the setting 'from within.'	**Parents are supporters** Parents support a setting 'from the outside' when called upon.	**Non-participatory parents** Actively seek not to be involved. Passively allow themselves to not be involved.

Why have you chosen these approaches and styles? Be specific with examples of what has informed your decision.

What messages might this have for practice and for trust?

What would you change (if anything) and why?

Can you identify areas for whole-school development here?

REFERENCES

Baier, A. (1986). Trust and antitrust. *Ethics*, 96(2), 231–260.

Baier, A. (1994). *Moral prejudices*. London: Harvard University Press.

Biesta, G.J.J. (2013). *The beautiful risk of education*. Oxon: Routledge.

Campagne, R.L., Dirks, K.T., Knight, A.P., Crossley, C. and Robinson, S. L. (2020). On the relation between felt trust and actual trust: examining pathways to and implications of leader trust meta-accuracy. *Journal of Applied Psychology*, 105(9), 994–1012.

Choi, J. (2017). Why I'm not involved: parental involvement from a parent's perspective. *Phi Delta Kappan*, 99(3), 46–49.

Cruz, J.D. (2019). Humble trust. *Philosophical Studies*, 176, 933–953.

Curtis, B.R. (2011). *Psychology of trust*. New York: Nova Science Publishers, Incorporated.

Fisher, A. and Tallant, J. (2020). Trust in education. *Educational Philosophy and Theory*, 52(7), 780–790.

Friere, P. (1994, reprinted in 2014). *Pedagogy of hope*. London: Bloomsbury Revelations.

Goodall, J. (2018). Learning-centred parental engagement: Freire reimagined. *Educational Review*, 70(5), 603–621.

Hallam, P.R., Dulaney, S.K., Hite, J.M. and Smith, H.R. (2014). Trust at ground zero: trust and collaboration within the professional learning community. In D. Van Maele, P.B. Forsyth, and M. Van Houtte (eds), *Trust and school life: the role of trust for learning, teaching, leading, and bridging*. London: Springer, 145–170

Hawley, K. (2014). Trust, distrust and commitment. *Noûs*, 48(1), 1–20.

Henderson, A.T., Mapp, K.L., Johnson, V.R. and Davies, D. (2007). *Beyond the bake sale: the essential guide to family school partnerships*. New York: The New Press.

Pugh, G. and De'Ath, E. (1989). *Working towards partnership in the early years*. London: National Children's Bureau.

Riley, K.A. (2017). *Place, belonging and school leadership: researching to make the difference*. London: Bloomsbury Academic.

Roberts, W. (2017). Trust, empathy and time: relationship building with families experiencing vulnerability and disadvantage in early childhood education and care services. *Australasian Journal of Early Childhood*, 42(4), 4–12.

Rogers, C. (1951, reprinted 2003). *Client-centred therapy: its current practice, implications and theory*. London: Constable and Robinson Ltd.

Schweizer, A., Niedlich, S., Adamczyk, J. and Bormann, I. (2017). Approaching trust and control in parental relationships with educational institutions. *Studia Paedagogica*, 22(2), 97–115.

Solvason, C., Cliffe, J. and Bailey, E. (2019). Breaking the silence: providing authentic opportunities for parents to be heard. *Power and Education*, 11(2), 191–203. https://doi.org/10.1177/1757743819837659.

Solvason, C. and Kington, A. (2019). Collaborations: providing emotional support to senior leaders. *Journal of Professional Capital and Community*, 5(1), 1–14. https://doi.org/10.1108/JPCC-05-2019-0010.

Solvason, C., Webb, R. and Sutton-Tsang, S. (2020). Evidencing the effects of maintained nursery schools' roles in early years sector improvements. Available from: https://tactyc.org.uk/research/.

Solvason, C., Hodgkins, A. and Watson, N. (2021). Preparing students for the 'emotion work' of early years practice. *NZ International Research in Early Childhood Education Journal*, 23(1), 14–23.

Somekh, B. (1994). Inhabiting each other's castles: towards knowledge and mutual growth through collaboration. *Educational Action Research*, 2(3), 357–381.

Tschannen-Moran, M. (2014). *Trust Matters: Leadership for Successful Schools*. Somerset: John Wiley and Sons Incorporated.

Webster, R.S. (2018). Being trustworthy: going beyond evidence to desiring. *Educational Philosophy and Theory*, 50(2), 152–162.

Wilson, T. (2018). *How to develop partnerships with parents: a practical guide for the early years*. London: Routledge.

CHAPTER 4
Allow Emotions

Johanna Cliffe

It goes without saying that emotions are part of us, they are part of the human condition whether we like it or not. Solomon (2007, p.1) goes as far as to say, "we live our lives through our emotions, and it is our emotions that give our lives meaning". However, knowing that they are an innate part of being human: something we *all* must contend with, does not make them any easier to deal with in daily practice. Emotions can be unpredictable, even horribly messy at times. I know that all of you reading this will be aware that when we discuss emotions, it is not just about dealing with children's emotions, as practitioners we manage our *own* emotions, the emotions of colleagues, the emotions of the children in our care and the emotions of the families we work with. Even with the best will in the world, and on the best day, dealing with more extreme emotions can be a challenge.

> I remember when I was in my first year of teaching and just about treading water in an extremely demanding school in an area of poverty. During one team meeting it was discussed that we would be introducing a new reading scheme in my year group. It was the final straw for me. I (totally irrationally) burst into tears. Over the next few days my wonderful, caring head teacher, tried to break it to me that I was perhaps a little stressed.
>
> *Carla*

In our previous work (Cliffe and Solvason, 2020, p.9), we discussed that it is not only the emotions that are more negatively perceived

DOI: 10.4324/9781003191209-4

that can be seen as an issue, but even excesses of more positive emotions are sometimes discouraged. In fact, in Western settings and classrooms, passionate behaviour of any kind is actively discouraged, not only with an eye to behaviour management but also so as not to detract from the extremely *serious* business of learning. As a parent I found this troubling and as an educator I feel no different. Eccelstone and Hayes (2019, p.vii) argue that this stifling of emotions in our children is the reason behind the so-called 'snowflake generation'; the idea that children in the 21st century require more support with managing their feelings than any other generation. We could spend the remainder of this book exploring possible reasons for the deterioration in children's mental and emotional health in the 21st century; and it is highly probable that the role that 24:7 connection to social media plays would be a key feature of that discussion, however, let's not get distracted, let's stick with the task in hand and continue to explore the role that emotions play within relationships in educational contexts.

Within our settings it is not just the emotions of children that are discouraged, we frequently feel uncomfortable with emotional responses from parents or colleagues, too. When we have to face that parent who arrives at the setting angry and upset because her child has been 'dropped down' an ability set, for example. As a parent, you can totally empathise with that emotion, but as practitioners we sometimes feel unable to express *our own* emotions for fear of being judged as unprofessional. As practitioners there is the expectation that we remain emotionally detached, yet Niesche and Haase (2012, p.271) argue that "good leadership" is often synonymous with not just "managing emotions" but "making emotions visible". So just what is the *right* approach to emotion?

There is no doubt that the emotional aspect of teaching can sometimes be exhausting it can sometimes feel like navigating a minefield. Hochschild (2012, p.102) coined the term "emotional labour" when discussing the kind of work people in caring professions, including education, undertake around 'managing' emotions. Hochschild argues that emotional labour is present any time you are "face-to-face and in voice-to-voice contact with the public". It is easy to forget this, and that for the education professional that means every minute of the working day (unless they manage to squeeze in a loo break at some point, which is far trickier than those outside of education will ever realise). Working with young children you have to *give* constant professional love, care, and attention. This means that at the end of particularly trying days it can feel that there is very little left for those at home that we care about most. I'm sure that many practitioners have had days when they've felt that their own children were getting short-changed because of their job.

The terms burn-out and "compassion fatigue" are used by Taggart (2013) and Hodgkins (2019, p.48) to accurately describe how many of us involved in education and care have felt at times. This is an aspect of the practitioner role that requires a whole host of skills that, as Niesche and Haase (2012) observe, it is highly unlikely that you were taught during your preparation for your role. And I'm not suggesting this is an inadequacy that is unique to *you*, you'll find no 'holier than thou' in this book, oh no; it applies to all of us involved in the complex business of educating and caring for others. So based on the premise that for many of us our 'emotion training' is limited (if there are any psychotherapists reading this, I sincerely apologise, you can probably skip the rest of this section), this chapter considers the power of emotions and how, for successful partnership working as well as successful interactions with children, we might find ways to make our emotions and emotional responses more visible. In this chapter I encourage you to be curious and respectful about emotions, and to explore what displays of emotions, expressed within those heightened moments, might actually be communicating underneath the tears or the raised voices.

RATIONAL AND IRRATIONAL EMOTIONS

Emotions are something that each one of us are born with: the capacity to *feel*. They are a natural and innate part of what it is to be human, yet in many respects emotions have become viewed as problematic within Western culture. With our innately British, 'stiff upper lip' approach, expressive emotions tend to be viewed as socially and culturally inappropriate. As Orphan (2004, p.106) stated, in Britain we are just "not very good at managing feelings".

This can result in a tendency for some to avoid emotional connections and employ shielding strategies, which might be misconstrued by others involved as not caring, or not listening.

REFLECTION POINT

When some people become emotionally overwhelmed, instead of erupting they can burrow deep inside themselves in an attempt to disconnect from the emotion involved. They can (outwardly) act as if the event never happened. This is because they cannot process the intensity of the emotions at that point and need time to process the situation slowly, bit by bit, which could take days. This means that when they are ready, they might randomly refer back to an incident that happened days and days ago and want to discuss it then. Which can seem extremely strange if you are on the receiving end.

How do you handle situations that you find emotionally overwhelming?

Paradoxically, despite this repression, educators are expected to be innately compassionate and to express empathy towards others (Hodgkins, 2019). Hodgkins (2019, p.48) explains that the constant and unrelenting nature of this can sometimes be overwhelming for the practitioner. Because of our tendency to stifle emotion, as practitioners we mostly manage our emotions alone, not sharing this aspect of our practice with colleagues (at least, not to the extent that we share other information) and certainly not with the parents that we interact with. Yet we all know the myriad of emotions that are involved in raising children. How many times have you heard a friend sob about a lack of instruction book for parenting following their latest parenting gaff? Parenting is an emotional rollercoaster, and by working with their children you are joining them for the ride. How we, as educators, deal with emotions – our own and those of others – will depend on our values, beliefs, culture, and status. It is important not to ignore or underestimate the impact of emotion within our daily practice.

Although we may not be consciously aware of it, emotions are political, and the way we consider emotions as a society, as a setting, even as an individual, can become a question of social justice; what emotion is given voice and what is silenced? Within various environments, what emotions are we *allowed* to show? As Cliffe and Solvason (2020, p.7) explain, in the Western world we attribute a hierarchy to emotions based on the ones that we are *comfortable* with: happiness, love, excitement, and joy (but these should also be demonstrated in moderation); and those we are less *comfortable* with, such as anger and sadness. Stenberg (2011, pp.349–50) suggests that emotions that are more uncomfortable, those considered socially unacceptable or inappropriate in certain contexts (however understandable they might be), are often 'written off' or labelled 'irrational'. Unhelpfully, this is further compounded by the notion that demonstrating these unreasonable emotions is a sign of *inferior* rationality and it is most often applied to marginalised groups such as women and children. So, it is vital that we consider what cultural norms we are buying into and whether some should be questioned.

As Solomon (2007) argues, there is a 'place' and a purpose for all emotions, extreme or otherwise, irrational or otherwise. It is through our experience of emotions that we grow as individuals, developing our social connections and our own foundations of wellbeing. Solomon (2007, p.72) continues that despite Western cultural constraints, "grief, laughter and happiness … are most meaningful when they are shared". Emotions provide us authentic ways with which to 'connect' with each other. This is just as relevant in education as it is in our personal lives. Solvason and Proctor (2021) note in their research that when parents of children with SEND receive their child's initial diagnosis they can feel sadness, anger, and grief, and this "emotional turmoil" as one teacher explains, can feel as though it has "blown their lives apart" (ibid., p.13). Yet Solvason and Proctor (ibid.) also refer to the '"fake smile" that many struggling parents use to mask their struggles, meaning that they can remain unshared. As practitioners it is important to be sensitive to the emotions that may lay just below the surface.

In Chapter 1 we referred to Orphan (2004, p.98), who honestly shares that having a child can make "you aware of feelings inside yourself that you had no idea existed, such as uncontrollable rage, sorrow, or a deep sense of joy". This is something that all parents can relate to, yet as parents in Western society we are expected to manage these emotions, as to display them might cause discomfort to others. Therefore, when we receive a sharp comment, or even an eye roll or a sigh from a disgruntled parent, this may well be just the tip of the iceberg in terms of their emotional wellbeing. What a parent may actually be saying, in the only way that they feel *allowed*, is: 'life is hard right now and I am only just treading water; as one human being to another, please, just give me a break'. Consider this and make a conscious effort during such moments to respond kindly. Just a 'how are things? Are you okay?' could make the world of difference to somebody.

Although it is a rare occurrence, it is perfectly understandable (and *should* be perfectly acceptable) when parents do express more extreme emotions. Although it may be difficult to be on the receiving end as an practitioner, it is entirely reasonable for a parent to react with anger, fear, or sadness to your suggestion that their child has behaved inappropriately or that they may have an additional need. It is natural for a parent to respond with irritation when their child has been injured (and yes, a scraped knee counts as injured when it is your own child) while playing in your care. The parent has entrusted their precious child to your safe-keeping and at that moment they feel let down, betrayed. And, as Carla mentioned in the previous chapter, that doesn't change as a child gets older, as parents we still want to fiercely protect our child. As a parent I distinctly remember the moment I confronted my son's secondary school over a long-term situation which I felt was causing him emotional harm and, therefore, was causing me a great deal of anger, frustration, and upset. The teacher's reaction made it clear that I was considered irrational and challenging because I had shared my viewpoint in an email complaint that was "quite strong". Too right it was strong ... my son's needs were being ignored and I needed to find a way of being heard if I was to protect him, I was communicating that this situation was not okay. In that moment I needed them to help me solve this problem that was causing my son (and so me) real distress; I needed them to step up and deal with the situation rather than ignoring it. It is really important, as practitioners, that we validate, rather than dismiss, the emotions of parents.

Hochschild (2012, p.32) notes that one way to deal with unexpected emotional encounters is to remind ourselves that we do not know what is happening for the other person in the interaction. It may sound simple, but in the heat of the moment this is not easy. Carla shared with me her embarrassment at ranting at a dentist's receptionist for not helping her son when he was in pain, only to discover that her son had only given a partial telling of the story and that the dentist had done all that they possibly could. She had to apologise for being a mother bear, made all the more embarrassing because her son was 21 at the time. Intensity of feeling comes with the parenting territory. And while it might not fix the situation itself, showing a willingness to hear parents without judging, to validate what may be a perfectly reasonable response to an extremely challenging situation, might make a huge difference to them. Being willing to 'sit' in those uncomfortable feelings with a parent, a colleague, or a child, tells them that it is okay, you are listening, and that they are not alone.

Some days, as we have all experienced, emotions are just too much, we are just too tired. Remember, this is the case for parents, too; we are all just people muddling through as best we can. So why, when it all feels so hard is it better to 'deal in', and allow emotions to emerge rather than keeping them buried? Rautamies et al. (2019, pp.897–8) suggest that for both the practitioner and the parent (and we can include children in this, too) there is a link between agency and emotions. The way that we feel, and the strength of those feelings, directly impacts how we take action within the different spheres of our lives. Emotions empower us (or sometimes overpower us). Stenberg (2011, p.351) asserts that the value of emotions within encounters is of the greatest importance, and that without emotions we "impoverish our own understanding of how we come to orientate ourselves to one another in the world around us". Within practitioner–parent relationships, how we acknowledge emotions and orient ourselves towards one another can result in empowering the practitioner *and* parent, or it can create resistance, dysfunction, disillusionment, and distrust. It goes without saying that either option has significant implications for outcomes for children.

REFLECTION POINT

Consider the following reflective questions and record the emotions that you felt and how this impacted on your actions and your relationships and interactions.

- Think of a time in your professional life when you have felt an extreme emotion, such as frustration, anxiety, grief, or shame. Record the situation that caused you to feel this way, and what happened. Pay attention to your feelings, how this impacted on your actions and how others responded to you.
- Repeat the above process, however this time consider a professional situation that involved expressing joy, pleasure, satisfaction, or excitement. Again, record the situation that caused you to feel this way, and what happened. Pay attention to your feelings, how this impacted on your actions, and how others responded to you.
- Finally, think about a time in your professional role where you felt unable to express an extreme emotion. Repeat the process. Reflect on what (or who) made the difference between the situations and their outcomes.

Having completed the exercise what clues do you feel this might hold for understandings around emotions and agency? Why might this be important within your practice?

EMPATHY AND COMPASSION FOR SELF AND OTHERS

Within education and care we know our daily roles consist of three types of activity: physical, mental, and emotional, or the management of feelings. These feelings can be our own, our colleagues', parents', or children's (Hochschild, 2012). When we "sign-up" to become practitioners there is an assumed understanding that we will be implicitly kind, warm, caring, and nurturing (Morris, 2020, p.3) and "outlaw" emotions as previously described by Stenberg (2011), are side-lined. We are expected to embody empathy and compassion in a bid to connect emotionally with those around us, to understand behaviour and the feelings that drive the actions and reactions, our own and others (Prowle and Hodgkins, 2020). Yet there is no training manual for any of this.

Hodgkins (2019) describes the concept of advanced empathy working in caring professions, which she sums up as *just knowing*. Within advanced empathy, working practitioners cultivate conscious awareness of hidden emotional states and what these might be communicating. It is about using all of our senses to consider the person in front of us, whether that is parent, colleague, or child and to seek to understand both visible and invisible emotional responses within the interaction. So, for example, reading the sharp comments of a parent as a sign of exhaustion or upset and reacting accordingly. Empathy itself is defined by Hodgkins (2019, p.46) as "the ability and willingness to understand another's thoughts, feelings, and struggles from their point of view". Similarly, Belzung (2014, p.178) defines it as "identifying oneself with someone else" through projecting ourselves into the situation and taking account of how we might feel and react, the decisions we might take. Belzung (ibid) further discusses the idea that there is a mirroring quality to empathy, for example if you are sitting across from a disgruntled parent, you might find yourself feeling similarly disgruntled quite quickly. On the other hand, if you hear a child let loose with a proper, belly laugh, then it is easy for your mood to lighten at this cheerful sound. Often these responses are subconscious, although I would task you to consider them more consciously, as this can provide interesting reflections and insight into which emotions we allow and feel comfortable with in different situations and how this affects our interactions.

Compassion is closely linked to empathy. Prowle and Hodgkins (2020, p.4) define compassion as feeling *for* another person, whereas Neff (2011, p.61) defines it as "suffering *with*" another. Neff (ibid) suggests that compassion implies recognition of the fact that we are all in this together, circumstances, experiences, and emotions that arise out of the messiness of life are all part of the human condition. Quite simply it reminds us that none of us are perfect and that we are all doing the best we can. Compassion in education and care lays the foundation for common ground, where we can appreciate ourselves, our colleagues, parents, and children rather than defaulting to judgement, which creates feelings of inadequacy and failure. The difference between care and compassion, and why one does not assume the other, is, as Taggart (2013) suggests, that compassion enables us to see and respect the *vulnerability* in someone else and to be moved to alleviate it while protecting their rights and their dignity. No small task, really, when you consider it.

Parents of children with SEND can be particularly vulnerable. Solvason and Proctor's (2021) research shared the range of emotions, including frustration, anger, fear, tiredness, desperation, distrust, disillusionment, and shame that parents of children with SEND often felt. The work of both Rogers (2011, p.572) and Solvason and Proctor (2021) describes how many parents of children with SEND feel they are constantly in a battle, or a "survival exercise", even before normal levels of family and work life stresses are factored in. They can feel beleaguered and isolated and can be left reeling from seeing their child set up to fail again and again within the schooling system while waiting for the appropriate support (Solvason and Proctor, 2021, p.7). So, it is perfectly understandable that they can bring all of this with them when they turn up at the classroom door. Therefore, think carefully about how you greet them ... is it with 'how are you doing?' or is it with 'has Sammy remembered their reading book today?'. Value them as people. I remember distinctly a parent sharing that they had been told that their child had been 'ok' with a hand wave, or a 'thumbs down' for a 'bad day'. This had been wholly disheartening for them, as they never had the pleasure of hearing about any positive moments within their child's day. Just take a moment and think about the number of times that you make contact with parents because there are issues that need discussing, compared to the amount of times that you share a positive moment, celebrate with parents, and inspire a little joy and hope.

My own research over recent years has made me aware of the many opportunities that I missed, whilst working in education, to brighten a parent's day by sharing with them a positive aspect of their child. I'm not saying that it never happened, I wasn't an emotionless monster, I'm just saying that I should have done it far more. Because it's an easy thing to do that not only increases your own joy through sharing it, but also the joy of the parent and child.

Carla

Developing empathy is a careful balance. Whilst constantly being placed in the position to hear the emotional communications of others can allow practitioners' "empathic senses to develop" (Prowle and Hodgkins, 2020, p.6), the tension remains of how they then manage this. The emotional price tag for being a practitioner is not recognised, particularly in a society that favours "reason over emotion" (Andrew, 2015, p.353), and where policies designed with safeguarding in mind have merely served to promote more "emotionally sterile" settings and classrooms (Morris, 2020, p.8). Hochschild (2012, p.102) coined the term "emotional labour" to describe the toil of continually managing empathy, as well as other emotions, whilst working in the caring professions.

We can probably all remember times when we have taken our work home, worrying about our students and their families in our own family time, away from the setting. I distinctly remember seeing one of the neglected children from my class near my home in just flimsy pumps, with bare legs, when the street was thick with snow. I agonised for days over what I should have done. When you work with children (and parents) as Elfer (2012, p.130) points out, you are expected to look perpetually cheerful and have "endless patience". This is the case regardless of what is going on in your own life. However, if we are to shoulder the responsibility for emotion work in daily practice, we *must* be self-compassionate, we must practice self-care, or, as Prowle and Hodgkins (2020, p.7) put it, "put our own oxygen mask on before helping others". We all know the phrase about treating others as we would wish to be treated, but sometimes we are guilty of sacrificing our own needs for others. Yes, compassion needs to be offered to those we work with, but it is equally vital that we save a healthy dose for ourselves.

ADDRESSING BLAME

Within a culture of scrutiny and judgement it is unsurprising that practitioners can sometimes feel compelled to safeguard their own practice by blaming parents; or that parents can sometimes defend their parenting by blaming educators. Hochschild (2012) suggests that we should be more mindful of this propensity and when we feel angry or frustrated by someone, we should try to seek out something positive in our own minds. Try to redirect an irritated, knee-jerk response to an irascible parent, to thoughts such as 'I can see you are doing your best, I know you love your child, you juggle so much, it must be tough for you at the moment'. Try to shift your thinking to see the parent as simply human, muddling through. So instead of "Katie doesn't have her PE kit *again*" try "PE is a bit tricky for Katie without her kit, would it be helpful for you if we sorted out some spare kit for her to keep at school?". A simple mental shift allows emotions to move through us, through the frustration or anger (however justified at that moment) to really see the person and show compassion to their situation.

When families experience vulnerability, and this could be just when bringing their child to your setting in the first place, it is natural for them to view this through their previous interactions, which may not have been positive. Within the research of Solvason and Proctor (2021), Roberts (2017), and Rogers (2011) a common theme is parents feeling judged, criticised, stigmatised, and deskilled in the eyes of educators, when what they are actually seeking is social connection, affirmation, and reassurance. One practitioner within Roberts' (2017, p.8) research noted that the best way to provide these things is to simply be "a real person". Likewise, Solvason and Proctor (2021) mentioned being 'real' with parents; they stress that there are occasions where we need to step outside of the role of 'expert' and just live the role of an authentic human being. As one of Solvason and Proctor's (2021, p.12) teachers suggested, sometimes we need to "put our egos to one side", after all "It's not about us, it's about this little person and that life".

Carla shared the difference that it made to her own and her son's school experience when she felt that the teacher really listened to her knowledge of her son and took this into account in her interactions with him. She explained how her son's insecurity, and defensiveness as a result, made him appear obnoxious. After many years of him being generally disliked by teachers Carla arranged to speak with his new teacher at the start of the year and explained the vicious circle of him behaving obnoxiously because he was insecure – then teachers disliked him because he seemed obnoxious – then he knew the teachers disliked him so that made him more insecure – and so more obnoxious, and so on. Carla said that this was the best year that her son ever had in primary school, no problems at all, because the teacher had genuinely listened and understood how challenging the situation had been for her son and changed the way that she dealt with him to focus upon the positives. He bloomed. One conversation changed the entire year.

Listening with an open heart, which can be empowering for both parties, is about learning to *lean into* the positive elements of the emotional work that we do. No matter how rubbish a day we may be having, we can all take a minute to put a smile on a parent's face by sharing in the joy of their child. In the research by Solvason, Webb, and Sutton-Tsang (2020), one practitioner even talked about 'embellishing the truth' a little on this front, because everyone wanted to hear something positive about their child. Parents need to know that not only do we like children in general, but we like *their child*, that we understand them, that we enjoy our time with them.

Solvason and Proctor's (2021) educators talked about reframing what we say to turn negatives into positives. In their conversations with SEND teachers, one used the example of carefully changing the wording of "he sat in a puddle all day" to "today we explored water" to transmit positive rather than negative messages to parents. We should not underestimate the impact that our words can have upon parents, so choose them with extreme care if you are to build trust, security, and safety within the relationship.

REFLECTION POINT

Within our role as educators, we are often on the receiving end of a whole spectrum of emotions from parents and children. When considering emotions, it is important to know what you

---

feel comfortable with and what you find hard to deal with. For example, while we might understand a parent's anger or even a child's, if we are not comfortable with 'anger' ourselves then angry situations can make us feel out of control, uncomfortable, or threatened.

Consider the following and record how *comfortable* and how *prepared* you feel to deal with any of these categories of emotions in your interactions with parents, colleagues, and children. You could rate the examples using a traffic light system: green for totally confident, amber as not sure yet, and red as uncomfortable and not prepared. Note the ones that do make you feel uncomfortable, consider why this might be? Are there any other emotional situations you can think of that are not recorded in the table? What are these and how might you rate them?

Emotional Scenarios: An Interaction With a Parent ...

Where verbal anger, aggression, and/or frustration is expressed.	Where physical anger, aggression, and/or frustration is expressed.	Where they might be expressing their worries and concerns.	Where they might be tearful or emotional.
Who is experiencing anxiety and/or might be feeling insecure.	Who is accusatory or intimidatory in their manner.	Who might be extremely excitable, joyful, or happy.	Who might always be busy, stressed, and/or forgetful.
Who is always ultra-organised.	Who is (perceived as) overly protective.	Who is a qualified, educator, or other professional.	Who is perceived as disinterested.
Who doesn't seem to listen.		Who is considered judgemental or challenging (for example, sexist or racist).	

You might consider a similar exercise with children and the emotions and behaviours that may occur in practice. For example, how confident do you feel with the angry child, or the excitable child? And so forth.

By completing this exercise, it will allow you to see your own practice strengths and where you may still need training or support. This might mean speaking to experienced colleagues who feel more confident in areas where you feel less confident. Being open and honest with what we are 'okay' dealing with and what we are less 'okay' dealing with is a professional response, however uncomfortable it may feel.

EMOTIONAL COACHING

Knowing the importance of emotions and creating an environment that is a safe space for emotional work can be two very different things. Emotions are unpredictable and so is the emotion work that we do. Even tried-and-tested practice strategies may not work consistently in moments of heightened emotions. If you approach a difficult situation with the firm belief that you have all the answers and will control the situation, you are likely to come unstuck fairly quickly. The whole point with emotion work is that you may not always be able to *fix* the situation. While as educators we are notorious for needing to feel in control (come on, we are all educators, we can be honest here), the chances are that you will not be able to control the outcome of an emotional encounter; emotional interactions inevitably bring with them an element of the unknown.

Emotion work is tricky; however, part of feeling confident in these situations is knowing all the above and knowing that it is still okay. The only thing that you can control, at least to some extent, is your emotional response to the situation. Making space to hear parents, sharing their burden for a little while, and acknowledging the limitations of what you can and cannot change, is a healthy and strong way forward. Solvason and Proctor's (2021) practitioners discussed being transparent and respectful, checking in with parents following an incident to see if they are 'happy' with the way it was handled, or if they would like you (as educator) to take a different approach next time. Simply allowing parents to know they are not alone and that you respect their view as the person who knows their child best, can have far more impact than you realise.

With that in mind I want to share a few things that may be of practical help when 'on the front line'. Knowing how emotions work can support you when dealing with emotionally heightened moments. Rose, Gilbert, and Richards (2016, pp.14–15) draw on the work of Dan Siegel, employing the idea of the 'fist model' of the brain to explain what is happening when children (or adults) 'act out'. Bear with the Americanisms here. The basic premise is that if we see our brain as a fist: clenched together with the thumb tucked in under the fingers, this represents a calm, thinking, and connected brain. When we come under stress or feel threatened the messages that race to our brains are about preparing for action and, ultimately, survival. Rose, Gilbert, and Richards (2016) explain that in this moment our primary emotions (fear, anger, and so forth) are 'running the show', and the 'disconnection' to our ability to think rationally is akin to 'flipping our lids'. This is demonstrated by opening the fingers of the hand to show that the brain is no longer connecting in the same way. Rational messages can no longer be relayed. Essentially, until we feel safe and secure our lid will remain 'flipped', and our thinking and control of our actions will be impaired. Normal service is resumed when the brain becomes reconnected.

This simile is really useful for helping us to understand what is happening with children in those moments of challenging behaviour, they are distressed. Equally, this image can give us insights into what happens with us, as adults, when we 'lose the plot' and enter survival mode. Rose, Gilbert, and Richards

(2016, p.100) outline a three-step emotional coaching approach, especially for dealing with such situations in educational environments. The steps are:

1. Recognise, empathise, validate, and label feelings.
2. Remind those involved of the limits of behaviour when everyone is calm (what is and is not okay).
3. Problem solve together; discuss what could be done next time and whether there is anything that needs to be done now to put things right.

Now obviously this needs a little fine tuning for working with parents, outlining rules of behaviour with them is probably not the best way to create a fruitful relationship. With adults it might be that you only need step one, to recognise, empathise, and validate feelings. A response along the lines of: "I can completely understand why you are feeling so angry, this situation is just not acceptable" is a good step towards defusing the situation. You might add step three when everyone is calm, making a plan together, or checking that parents agree with how you are approaching something. This not only allows parents to feel heard, it communicates that their view will be respected and acted upon. But we also recognise that on rare occasions you may need to set 'behavioural' limits. For example, to point out that whilst we might understand a parent's anger, it is upsetting for children to witness shouting or arguing between adults in their setting, which must remain, for them, a safe sanctuary; and that it would be far better if they entered the setting when they were ready to discuss an issue more rationally.

> One of my most distinct memories of my early teaching was the time when, whilst in the cloakroom with my class at the end of the day, a mother came in and heard from her son that he had been 'picked on' by another child. He was the type of child who relished the victim role (most situations were vastly exaggerated, if I'd asked him to pick up his pencil this would translate to him spring cleaning the entire classroom through

his break and lunchtime) and his mum was, I don't know how else to put this, as hard as nails, and mildly terrifying … particularly to my newly-qualified-teacher eyes. Her response to hearing that her son had been (supposedly) picked on again was to inform him extremely loudly, so that myself and all of the other children in the class could hear, that "next time it happens you just pick up a bleeping chair and smack the other kid around the bleeping head with it".

Did I have the 'now I understand you being upset' conversation with her? Did I 'eck! I just pretended that I hadn't heard it whilst ushering all of the other children out of the door. Maturity and experience have a considerable role to play in dealing with such situations. Thirty years of experience later I'd like to think that I could have that conversation … although if it were this particular parent, from what I remember of her, I may still avoid it and pass the issue on to a far braver superior.

Carla

As a strategy, Rose, Gilbert, and Richards' (2016) approach can be quite practical in the moment, but it does take practice. You are unlikely to get it right first time and it may not be a cure-all in every interaction. Empathy and compassion will still be needed and validating emotions may need to happen over and over before parents (or even you) feel calm and safe enough to step out of survival mode. The above may not be an easy 'answer' but it is a useful tool.

REFLECTION POINT

Think back to a situation in your own practice where you felt that your interaction with a parent was positive and productive. Make some notes on the following reflective points:

- What did you say and do that made it feel this way?
- What did the parent say and do that made it feel this way?

- What feelings do you think were present in that moment?
- How does this situation make you feel now?

Now think back to a time where you had a negative experience with a parent. Consider and make notes on the following:

- What was said and done by the parent within this situation?
- How did you respond?
- What do you think the parent might have been feeling?
- What did you know about their circumstances?
- What were you feeling?
- What was happening to you at this time?
- Do you feel that the emotional response of both yourself and the parent were 'justified'?
- If you could engage with this situation again, would you change anything? If yes, what and why?

PROFESSIONAL LOVE

This chapter cannot finish without a brief look at professional love. Professional love is not a term that everyone in the sector is entirely comfortable with. This can be recognised in the "no touch" policies (Morris, 2020, p.8) appearing in settings and the general culture of fear, that has arisen toward showing any physical affection. Whilst this veto on physical touch might be understandable, particularly with safeguarding in mind, it can present a moral and ethical dilemma regarding care and professional love within practice (Page, 2018) and particularly when dealing with the most young and vulnerable children. The constant balancing act that we undertake every day between *educating* and *caring* not only adds to the burden of emotional labour but places us in a dilemma with a view to approaching and acting within emotional moments. To be clear, I am not saying that we should not be sensible and professional as educators, the safeguarding of children is paramount (none of us need reminding how the cost of the inappropriate actions of a few, are felt by all within the education sector); however, professional love is a significant part of what we do, whether we give it this label or not.

Page (2018, p.126) describes professional love as "situated in the complex lives, experiences, attitudes, feelings. and histories of everyone in a setting" and comments that it is expressed as a willingness to engage with the *hard stuff* that permeates life. Showing kindness, empathy and compassion practically demonstrates a willingness to tackle that 'hard stuff', whether this is in partnership with children or their parents. Excluding the notions of professional love, compassion, and empathy from our educational policy attempts to keep the spheres of 'family and home' private and separate from the work of 'education' (Page, 2018, p.134). And you may feel this is exactly right and just as it should be. However, we know (and research has proven) that positive outcomes for children require a more holistic view, which includes knowledge of home and other areas of the children's lives. As one educator in Solvason and Proctor (2021, p.11) observed, we should not be left guessing what is happening in children's lives and how that is impacting upon them whilst they are with us, we should be asking, finding out "the context of how their weekend was, how they were this morning, things that might potentially be problematic during the day". We need to know the big stuff and the small stuff and yes even the in between stuff. To successfully work in partnership with parents requires us to understand who they are, where they are coming from, and what is going on for them and parents. We cannot do this without somehow bridging that divide between home and setting.

REFLECTION POINT

When working in early years, the book corner, for all children, was always the point where children *snuggled up*. I have lost count of the children that sat on my lap for story or snuggled in close as they sat beside me. One particular child always played with my hair as we read together. Many children seek physical comfort and security, not only when they have hurt themselves, when they are ill, or when they are missing home, but just as a natural facet of being a child. It is sad that these naturally occurring moments of connection are now frowned upon or viewed with fear and suspicion.

What are your thoughts on this and the concept of 'professional love'?

Care, historically, was seen as the mainstay of early education, remaining conspicuous by its absence from policy and rhetoric in the older age phases. Rouse and Hadley (2018) suggest that the homogenisation of education ensured care began to disappear, even from early education, in favour of future-focused, assessment-driven practice. The child's need for a caring pedagogy has not disappeared; it has merely been reduced to an undetermined, undervalued, underappreciated, and almost invisible emotional practice. Rouse and Hadley's (2018, p.159) suggestion that "learning should be seen in the context of care rather than care being seen in the context of learning" raises the question of whether, in the UK as well as other Western-based countries, we have our ideas about education backwards. Whether we should be reassessing our focus on professional love, care, empathy, and compassion, (just as the nursery practitioners quoted in Chapter 1 did) knowing that the learning will follow. Provision, whatever the level, is not just about filling learners with knowledge, it is about meeting physical, mental, and *emotional* needs, keeping individuals safe physically and *emotionally*. It is about professional love and being emotionally invested (Rouse and Hadley, 2018, p.160).

The different spheres of our lives are not separate; they interrelate and occasionally crash in upon one other, which undoubtedly has implications for professional relationships and the practitioner–parent–child dynamic. Allowing care, empathy, and compassion to become invisible erodes the power and the importance of our emotion work, which, however we look at it, is fundamental to what we do. Allowing ourselves to feel and express professional love encapsulates those approaches and meets parents and children in those messy and complex emotional spaces. Professional love is about 'doing the hard stuff', allowing emotions to flow in the hope that we can all feel just that little bit less alone in the business of educating and caring for children.

CONCLUSION

The purpose of this chapter was to explore the power of emotions, to consider why they are so important within education, and why we need to acknowledge them for successful partnership working. It recommended that we be curious and respectful about emotions, to find out what they might be communicating. This chapter considers why understanding the place of emotions and allowing them to flow is important within educational and caring relationships. It explains why emotions should remain visible and be embraced, even the ones that make us uncomfortable, or that are considered outlawed or irrational.

We have discussed strategies, such as emotion coaching, that can be practically helpful, but the key to emotion work remains firmly encapsulated in professional love and expressing empathetic and compassionate approaches. That we should be aware of ourselves and our emotional labour within our practice and make time to care for ourselves as well as others. We discussed how we need to empathise with where parents are coming from, be considerate of their hopes and fears for their children, and *lean into* the positive elements of the emotional work we do. It reminded us that taking a minute to make someone's day, by sharing in the joy of their child, is a magical moment that should not be taken for granted. It is a privilege to be a parent and a practitioner, and some of us are lucky enough to be both. However, that in no way discounts from the fact that both these roles can be incredibly tough. If we remember nothing else, we need absolutely and unequivocally to remember we are, for better or for worse, all in this together, on the bad days as well as the good, so act with kindness.

KEY POINTS TO TAKE AWAY FROM THIS CHAPTER

1. As a society we tend to suppress emotion, yet being a parent magnifies these feelings.
2. Emotional labour, as a practitioner, can be exhausting, this is something that our training does not prepare us for.
3. We have cultural norms which make us view certain emotions as irrational – therefore it is common for people to hide emotions behind a rational mask.
4. It is good to understand what happens in moments of extreme emotion, so that we can better deal with them.
5. Instead of reacting or being dismissive of extreme emotion from parents, try to *lean into* this and show understanding and kindness.
6. Consider your feelings about 'professional love'. It is useful to acknowledge that education and care embraces cognitive, physical, *and* emotional needs.

TEAM ACTIVITY

Emotion Work with Parents

This can be as formal and detailed or as ad hoc as you like. Think about your provision as you consider and complete these reflective questions and tasks relating to how you 'allow emotions' within your practice:

1. The next time you welcome parents into your setting do an internal 'emotion check' as they walk through the door:
   Suggested reflective questions to consider –
   What do you know about each parent and child?
   How do they 'look' this morning?
   What are they saying and what might they not be saying?
   How confident do you feel in working with them? Why?

2. Think about your current parent base:
   Suggested reflective questions to consider –
   Is there anyone you feel may need extra support? Why?
   Is anyone 'a challenge' to work with at the moment? Why?
   Do you need to find out more?

3. Consider your general daily practice with regard to emotional work:
Suggested reflective questions to consider –
Does your provision make time for parents to express how they feel and receive emotional support?
What does this look like?
Is it effective?
How do you know?
What else could you do?

4. Approaching difficult conversations:
Suggested reflective questions to consider –
How do you tackle different conversations? Think about your language, tone of voice, body language.
How do you contact parents or let them know you need to talk to them?
Where do these conversations take place?
What might this environment look and feel like to parents?

Emotion Work with Colleagues
5. Next time you are in work again do a 'self and colleague emotion check' and repeat this at various times during the day, this could be a visual and verbal check in.
Suggested reflective questions to consider –
How does each look and feel, what might their language, tone, body language, and actions be communicating? Why?
How does the provision 'feel'? Does it feel happy, busy, exciting, gloomy, noisy?
Is there any action that needs taking? If yes, what and why?

What Are Your Thoughts at This Point?

On a scale, that spans something like 'we do not support parents or colleagues with feelings and emotion work' to 'feelings and emotion work fully informs and is fully embedded in our practice' where do you think you would be?

Note: what *three* things are strengths, things you do well; and what *three* things would you like to change or improve? Rank these changes with regard to importance so you know what you might tackle first. Create an action plan with what to change, when, and how, include how you will know your change is effective.

REFERENCES

Andrew, Y. (2015). Why we feel and what we do: emotional capital in early childhood work. *Early Years International Research Journal*, 35(4), 351–365.

Belzung, C. (2014). Empathy. *Journal for Perspectives of Economic, Political, and Social Integration*, 19(1), 177–191.

Cliffe, J. and Solvason, C. (2020). The role of emotions in building new knowledge and developing young children's understanding. *Early Years International Research Journal*, 32(2), 129–141.

Eccelstone, K. and Hayes D. (2019). *The dangerous rise of therapeutic education*. Classic ed. Oxon: Routledge.

Elfer, P. (2012). Emotion in nursery work: work discussion as a model of critical professional reflection, *Early Years*, 32(2), 129–141.

Hochschild, A.R. (2012). *The managed heart: commercialization of human feeling, update with a new preface* (1st ed.). London: Berkeley.

Hodgkins, A. (2019). Advanced empathy in the early years – a risky strength. *NZ International Research in Early Childhood Education Journal*, 22(1), 46–58.

Morris, L. (2020). Love as an act of resistance: ethical subversion in early childhood professional practice in England. *Contemporary Issues in Early Childhood*, 22(2), 124–319.

Neff, K. (2011). *Self compassion*. London: Hodder and Stoughton.

Niesche, R. and Haase, M. (2012). Emotions and ethics: a Foucauldian framework for becoming an ethical educator. *Educational Philosophy and Theory*, 44(3), 276–288.

Orphan, A. (2004). *Moving on: supporting parents of children with SEN*. London: Fulton.

Page, J. (2018). Characterising the principles of professional love in early childhood care and education. *International Journal of Early Years Education*, 26(2), 125–141.

Prowle, A. and Hodgkins, A. (2020). *Making a difference with children and families: re-imagining the role of the practitioner*. London: Macmillan Education UK.

Rautamies, E., Vähäsantanen, K., Poikonen, P. and Laakso, M. (2019). Parental agency and related emotions in the educational partnership. *Early Child Development and Care*, 189(6), 896–908.

Roberts, W. (2017). Trust, empathy and time: Relationship building with families experiencing vulnerability and disadvantage in early childhood education and care services. *Australasian Journal of Early Childhood*, 42(4), 4–12.

Rogers, C. (2011). Mothering and intellectual disability: partnership rhetoric? *British Journal of Sociology of Education*, 32(4), 563–581.

Rose, J., Gilbert, L. and Richards, V. (2016). *Health and wellbeing in early childhood*. London: Sage.

Rouse, E. and Hadley, F. (2018). Where did love and care get lost? Educators and parents' perceptions of early childhood practice. *International Journal of Early Years Education*, 26(2), 159–172.

Solomon, R.C. (2007). *True to our feelings: what our emotions are really telling us*. New York: Oxford University Press.

Solvason, C. and Proctor, S. (2021). 'You have to find the right words to be honest': nurturing relationships between teachers and parents of children with special educational needs. *Support for Learning*, 36(3), 470–485.

Solvason, C., Webb, R. and Sutton-Tsang, S. (2020). What is left...?: the implications of losing maintained nursery schools for vulnerable children and families in England. *Children and Society*. https://authorservices.wiley.com/api/pdf/fullArticle/16752045.

Stenberg, S. (2011). Teaching and (re)learning the rhetoric of emotion. *Pedagogy*, 11(2), 349–369.

Taggart, G. (2013). The importance of empathy. *Nursery World*. Available from: https://www.nurseryworld.co.uk/Opinion/article/the-importance-of-empathy (accessed 9 June 2021).

CHAPTER 5
Tackling Difficult Conversations

Johanna Cliffe

I think it is fair to say that if you work in education and care (in any age phase) then you will know that difficult conversations are part of the territory. Yet, I am going to go out on a limb here and suggest that during your training you were probably *not* trained in how to navigate difficult conversations. You are not alone, I didn't have any training on this either, very few of us will have, even though it appears fairly obvious that tricky conversations are just as likely to be a part of the practitoner's role as they are for that poor person fielding complaints on a store's customer services desk. And these conversations can be really challenging, to the point that Whitaker and Fiore (2016, p.96) comment that "with our most challenging parents, we would schedule a root canal in lieu of meeting with them if we could".

I remember all my firsts, many of which I'd like to forget. For example, the first conversation with a parent to broach the subject of a referral for their child. I remember clearly staying with them through their rollercoaster of emotions which ranged from relief and validation, to anger, fear, and finally just tears. I remember the first unhappy parent who was both angry and terrified that I was going to speak to social services. Then there was the first time I had to tell a parent their child was hurt in my care; they had been bitten by another child who didn't want to share a toy, so yes, properly hurt. I also remember the time I had to mention to a parent that the heated discussion that she and her partner had had at home the night before had been overheard and retold, word perfectly, including many intimate details that I really did not need to know, by their darling child. I also remember the rest of the staff's sharp exit, as no one wanted a part of *that* conversation. Excellent recall on the part of the child, though. Every cloud and all that. After each one I remember thinking

DOI: 10.4324/9781003191209-5

'what if?' What if I had approached it differently? Did I say the right things? Had I done the right things? Had I done enough? Despite time and experience the reality is that these emotive conversations do not get any easier. Knowing that what you are about to say is likely to upset someone is never a good place to be.

No matter how many difficult conversations you've already had, there will still be times when you will see a parent coming and your stomach will flip because you know *just* how awful the conversation is likely to be (and yes, point taken, I probably need to reread the 'never assume' chapter). When you know that these conversations are coming, you can spend hours overthinking them, running through scenarios that *might* occur and what you *might* say. And then there are those conversations, as articulated in Solvason and Proctor (2021, p.13), the ones where you know that a parent is hanging in there by the skin of their teeth, and you are about to deliver the straw that broke the camel's back. It is these last conversations that left me soul searching every time. I know from my own experience, from colleagues who have children with SEND, parents who I have worked with and from experiences drawn from research, that these are the moments parents are most vulnerable. It is at these times that parents cling to and "remember every word" (The National Federation of Voluntary Bodies, 2007, p.7), every gesture; they will remember your kindness, compassion and sincerity *or* your insensitivity for life. Remember Carla's clear recount of the teacher's tirade against her son over 15 years ago. These moments can leave scars, and this is a responsibility that none of us should take lightly.

REFLECTION POINT

What do difficult conversations mean to you as a practitioner?

Spend a few minutes considering this question and then reflect on those below within the context of your workplace.

- What is your experience of difficult conversations so far?
- List the different difficult conversations you have had. (If this would take a few hours, choose a few that most stick in your memory.) Why did they happen? How did they go?

- Can you identify why they went the way that they did?
- How do you feel when you think about them? Why might this be?
- Was there anything you would change? Why?

There is no quick fix or easy answer here, life is messy and difficult conversations are … well … difficult. Parents, like all human beings, can be challenging, and our unease does not lessen with the frequency of difficult conversations that we have with certain families, even if it is on a daily basis. However, as Whitaker and Fiore (2016) remind us, parents are crucial sources of information, help, and potential support; in essence they are a resource (just as we are) for their children and their learning, even those that we find most challenging to engage with. If you compare it to a puzzle, as adults we all hold pieces of the puzzle that makes up the child's life experience, and without every piece of the picture it remains incomplete. Therefore, despite the nausea and the sweaty palms, we navigate these conversations as best as we can, because we know that they need to happen. Yet, as you will notice with many of the recurring themes within this book, knowing something needs to happen is a completely different ball game from making sure that it does actually happen, and as successfully as possible. This chapter, therefore, explores what we can do to best navigate the potentially choppy waters of difficult conversations. Because avoiding parents and the horror of the ensuing interaction, however tempting, does not work. Instead, we need to "lean into" vulnerability (Brown, 2018, p.4) and use this as a strength to build positive, trusting relationships within the work that we do.

WHY SHOULD WE HAVE DIFFICULT CONVERSATIONS?

In theory it is good to have a conversation before it becomes a confrontation, although it goes without saying that the difficult conversation can *become* a confrontation. In most cases, you'll be damned if you do and damned if you don't, so it's best to just get it over with. Some people (notice I didn't say parents, they are not a special breed, this is about everyone) are just plain difficult, full stop. As Whitaker and Fiore (2016, p.111) described them, these "most challenging people just throw stuff at a wall (or at you) to see if it sticks". The conundrum here is that these are often the people who are most in need of your support. And in attempting to offer that support you will put yourself in a precarious position. But, as Brown (2018, p.15) stated, "you can't get to courage without a rumble with vulnerability". And we have already discussed the relationship between vulnerability and trust in Chapter 3.

It now seems slightly cliché to say that the worst behaviours are a cry for help, but it also becomes much easier to deal with others if we understand behaviours in this way. I remind my students regularly that all behaviour is communication; the more expressive the behaviour the greater the emotion (for example frustration, anger, or fear) demonstrated. The more that emotion cannot be communicated in a healthy way, the more communication becomes *stuck*, and the greater the *vulnerability* of those involved. This is the same whether it is a child, a parent, or a colleague, and regardless of why the vulnerability is there, the important thing is that we see it, we see them and we hear what they are trying to convey.

Difficult conversations are vital in partnership working because they help to build trust and respect, as both parties (practitioners and parents) show a willingness to deal with the hard stuff, to experience relational vulnerability. As practitioners we don't have all the answers, and honestly I don't think we are expected to, but what we can do is be present and listen, to sit with a parent, a child, right there in the moment, in the messiness of life and engage in professional love and compassion (Page, 2018). Brown (2018, p.162) articulates this as "showing up and being courageous". We may not have all the answers, but the aim of a productive dialogue is that you try to work it out together.

FIRM FOUNDATIONS

The knack, according to Whitaker and Fiore (2016, p.64), is to communicate well when the going is good so that the groundwork is there, and relationships are established for when you really need them. Seems quite simple so far, doesn't it? When things go wrong or situations become complex and/or perplexing for the myriad reasons that they do, then parents will know you, they will know that you are good at your job (and, perhaps more importantly, that you have an interest in them as a human being, that you care) and rational communication will ensue. At least that is the theory. Having had many difficult conversations as a a practitioner and as a parent I know, just as you know, no magic happens in the heat of the moment, difficult conversations are at best uncomfortable and at worse explosive.

Vuorinen (2021) suggests that knowing each other well has both benefits and pitfalls. Developing daily communications with parents *should* lead to mutually beneficial, strong, and trusting relationships. Chappel and Ratliff's (2021, p.19) research identified that what parents valued most within any communication with practitioners was that it was personalised. Although this research was conducted in schools in Hawai'i, there is no reason at all why things would not be the same in the UK. Personalisation can only happen when time has been taken to get to know individual children and individual families. Acknowledging parents on a daily basis can be one way of approaching this, and beneficial in building rapport. I remember being on 'door duty' every morning to meet and great every child and parent at the beginning and end of the day, engaging in informal chats during drop-off and pick-up times. This helped me to *know* my parents and *know* my children, and for them to *know* me, and they seemed to really appreciate that acknowledgement and that brief connection every day.

However, a simple beginning and end-of-day strategy cannot work for all; these are busy times, and it may genuinely not be possible to engage with this effectively, or in a way that allows parents to see, hear, and feel your interest. In fact, Vuorinen (2021, p.2538) noted that it can be a time where you might actively avoid parent engagement, using the needs of the children in the moment as a kind of *cover* for not taking the time or the responsibility for speaking to particular (or all) parents. Now it might be that your current cohort of children do genuinely need you at these times

---

and therefore drop-off and pick-up times do not work for you in your provision. Or, it may be like those parents in Solvason and Proctor's (2021) research where the children are bussed to school and no face-to-face dialogue happens with parents at all. Whatever your context, it is worth considering *how* and *when* you can be available to parents in a more informal way and on a regular basis as the foundation in establishing a strong working relationship; so that you have this relationship to *fall back on,* if and when you may need to. There are more ideas about this back in Chapters 1 and 2.

REFLECTION POINT

How do you make time daily for parents to engage more informally with you?

Reflect on the above question and list specific times and/or strategies from your practice.

Do you feel these more informal occasions support you in building rapport with your parents? Why?

How do you feel this might support you when you have to discuss more difficult topics?

There can, of course, be disadvantages to a closer relationship with parents, in that the more we know about each other the more differences (or, even dislike) can emerge, and sometimes this can be a hindrance. When differences in values, culture, and parenting practices arise it can impact upon the way we see each other, and on the importance that we then attach to information given and received. A simple example that is likely to come up in any informal chat between parent and educator is the dreaded question from parents ,"do you have kids?" Now we all know that this is a no-win situation for the practitioner. Either you answer yes and are, therefore, expected to be more tolerant about every frustratingly difficult aspect of their child's behaviour because you are *in the know* with how difficult parenting can be, or you answer no, in which case you obviously do not have the first clue how difficult parenting can be. Either response is not helpful to *any* conversation, let alone a difficult one where your professional knowledge may not be respected in the light of either a lack of personal parenting experience or what is perceived as a cold lack of care.

Clearly it is not my intention to say we should *not* get to know the families we work with, or that daily communications and inter- actions are bad, just to point out that even when you do lay the groundwork and do everything right, you cannot always change the nature of difficult interactions. However, a stronger foundation is never going to hurt, because, as Whitaker and Fiore (2016, p.51) suggest, it "is a way to build and nurture credibility even with the most challenging of families".

It is worth pausing this chapter here and considering how you have approached reading this book. Carla and I won't judge for a minute if you have jumped into chapters that seem most relevant or interesting to you and have not read each in turn (we probably would have done the same). However, here I would say that many strategies that might support you in difficult conversations have already been mentioned in other chapters. For example, whenever you are dealing with tough topics there will always be emotions of one sort or another, therefore you might like to return to Chapter 4 which explores allowing emotions and consider the practical sug- gestions, particularly emotional coaching, moving forward. It also goes without saying that if we build relationships that are strong from the outset then difficult conversations will be approached more positively, from a position of mutual respect. For this aspect, Chapter 3, on trust, might offer insights that could be drawn upon. I have mentioned several times that all of us (me included) need many reminders from the "never assume" chapter (Chapter 2) and the importance of finding space to listen (Chapter 1). I won't repeat the advice given in those chapters here, but there are a few other areas to consider specific to this chapter which follow.

MIND YOUR LANGUAGE

The language that we use when broaching challenging topics can be of paramount importance. I have already mentioned the notion that what is said to parents when they are at their most vulnerable can stay with them with lasting effect (The National Federation of Voluntary Bodies, 2007). At these moments it is especially important not to patronise or demean. Jargon, acronyms, and unfamiliar turns of phrase, as pointed by Thompson (2018), can be damaging and serve to 'freeze parents out' of the conversation. Language that is pitched at inappropriate levels, either in tone or content, can serve to reinforce power differences and build barriers rather than helping to break them down. There is a need to find a way to explain any unfamiliar terms to parents and to meet them on a conversational level without slipping into belittling them. Not always an easy balance.

REFLECTION POINT

Activity 1

Consider for a moment a time where you had a conversation that you didn't understand. Maybe this was because of the language used, or perhaps the jargon or acronyms that you were not certain of. Reflect and write notes on how this made you feel.

Activity 2

List the different acronyms you use within your practice, a few to get you going might include, SEND and SENDco, SALT, EHCP, EAL. How often do you use these acronyms in your language with parents and in your reports? How do you ensure they understand these terms and what they mean?

However, there is even more to consider in terms of the way that we discuss children with parents in relation to the messages that we are sending. When we speak to parents we can, from what might appear necessity, become preoccupied with what we see to be the issues, the difficulties, the things that children cannot do, what we think is *wrong*. However well intended, and I do acknowledge that there is a time factor at play here, not only does this approach fail to respect the child in the situation, after all "a child is a person not just an object of concern" (Longley and Sharma, 2011, p.119), but it also takes a perpetually deficit approach which can wear parents down. This can particularly be the case where challenging behaviour is repeatedly being discussed.

Whitaker and Fiore (2016, p.56) argue that praise is more important than we realise, and that in our actions and our language we need to celebrate small steps in the right direction. In a recent study, funded by the Department for Education, Pen Green (2018, p.12) recommend reframing the way we approach parents of children with SEND to consider children's strengths and how we can support their achievements with the family. This can support a different and firmer-footed approach to difficult conversations. When framed in more positive language, harder-to-hear messages can be understood and accepted more easily, they are more palatable, although still just as honest, and promote more open conversation than deficit or lack approaches. Remember the PE kit conversation in Chapter 4, and how much more likelihood there is of a positive conclusion being reached if a conversation between practitioner and parent started with "Would it be helpful for Katie if we sorted her out some spare kit to keep in school?" instead of "Why does Katie never have her kit?".

This idea of taking a positive approach to difficult news brought to mind the experience of submitting articles for publication in journals. It is perfectly normal to receive a rejection, or a tonne of feedback on the ways that the article should be improved. This is something that I've gradually become used to, however the tone that the feedback is given in can vary enormously. Let's take for example the "we might publish this, but it needs lots of work" response. This will be couched in two possible ways: the first is the "let me demonstrate how much more intelligent I am than you by pointing out all of the amateurish failings in this piece of writing which make it unsuitable for a *serious* academic such as myself" approach. The second is the "this is great and a really important topic, let me suggest some ways that you might make it even better" approach. No one wants to be made to

> look stupid, or a failure, but everyone has room for improve-
> ment. How those areas for development are broached is key
> to a positive or negative experience on the part of the recipi-
> ent. And no prizes for guessing which of those journals I'd be
> more likely to submit future work to …
>
> *Carla*

When approaching difficult conversations, where possible, it is always useful to start with the parent and what they think and feel. For example, asking: "How do you feel James is settling in?" or "How do you think Sally is getting on?" This can sometimes open the door enough that parents can share their concerns in a way that may do all the hard work for you, particularly if they are already concerned about the very thing that you want to talk about. Even if this is not the case, you are showing them that their views, thoughts, and feelings carry weight, and that their voice is important.

Whilst not language as such, when we are in the moment, tackling the hard stuff with parents, we need to also be prepared to allow for some silences. However tempting it may be, avoid filling gaps in conversation with more information or explanation, because the parent may already be struggling to process the information given. Silences, as noted in Pen Green's (2018) research, can provide much needed time for parents to process, digest, and then formu-late responses to what might have been completely unexpected, or challenging information. Space and time to think can be more use-ful than you know, even though, as practitioners, we can become used to our own voices filling the days, and even when the silence may leave us squirming in discomfort. It reminds me of the 'count to ten in your head' rule that I so confidently advise practitioners to use with children, allowing the child time to process the informa-tion and formulate an answer, and that I should employ it myself more often.

Also, be prepared to repeat and revisit topics with parents over time. I recently watched a woman being interviewed who had received some awful news from the police about her daughter. She explained how she kept missing the key point that the police were telling her, because she simply was not able to process it. Just as the reflection point in the previous chapter highlighted, some parents will not be able to deal with the information given there and then. Some parents will need to go away and digest information before they are able to discuss it. Allow parents time and space if that is what they need.

REFLECTION POINT

Consider for a moment that you need to receive challenging news; think about how you would like to be told.

- How would you like the person to approach you?
- What tone of voice? What language? What body language?
- What environment would you like to be in?
- What would support you in hearing what you did not wish to hear?

Make notes. What might this tell us about sharing challenging news? What can we learn from this?

DIVERSITY AND DIFFERENCE CONVERSATIONS

It would be remiss in this chapter not to consider one final facet of conversation: diversity and difference. This is not so much a difficult conversation but can still feel daunting, or tricky. In a session with students recently we were discussing concepts such as privilege, equity, and equality. We talked about barriers that certain groups in society would face that we, as largely white, British, and middle class would be oblivious to. I shared my own experience of my parents being told by my (male) design technology teacher that I should not pursue architecture because it was 'not for girls'; and how I felt extremely uncomfortable at university having arrived from my working-class estate and comprehensive school, in a culture that was all privately schooled students and pads in London.

We discussed issues of gender, sexuality, disability, and poverty, but the topic that the students *all* felt was most difficult to tackle, day to day, was ethnicity. Unanimously they said that they avoided the topic because they felt that they had no knowledge and experience of it (so what right had *they* to discuss it?) but, most importantly, because they were terrified of saying the wrong thing. And it's no wonder. We live in a society where a manager in a multi-million-pound post can be sacked for saying 'coloured' instead of 'black'. So where do we start with tackling this? Well, as we have been saying all along, by not making presumptions, by taking interest, asking questions, and *really listening*.

So let's take as an example how we might broach traditional celebrations such as Mother's Day or Father's Day with a same sex couple. And what about extended families where there are parents and step-parents? Or kinship families where care is undertaken by a sibling, a grandparent, or a foster carer? Well, how about asking? One student described how a little girl in her setting had two male parents who she referred to as 'Dad' and 'Daddy'. Potential problem solved: "Who is collecting you tonight? Dad or Daddy?" But be aware that whilst open and honest communication is always best and would be how many of us would hope to deal with these potential tensions in practice, recent research by Leland (2021, p.161) suggests that not all same sex families are quite ready to have these conversations yet, and that we shouldn't force their hand. Like the student who still uses the term 'mum and dad' all the time, despite being in a lesbian relationship herself, there may be steps that are still a bit too far, so be careful to avoid bulldozing in, even if your intention is to do the right thing. We need to be aware that what seems pressing, or necessary to us, may not be a priority for the families that we work with. Be sure to see things from their perspective and follow their lead. And how do you do that? By asking and listening.

> I remember working with a family where I asked a mum if she could support us in learning and sharing Christmas songs in her family's native language. This was something that, at the time,

was recommended as a best practice strategy to support children in bridging the language gap in a fun and non-threatening way. However, the mum did not consider this appropriate, she stated clearly that her child came to the setting to learn English, and this is what she wanted. Her native language was for communication at home only.

We needed to respect the wishes of this parent, and it took many more *informal* interactions for us to build a stronger relationship where this could be revisited and discussed, and a compromise reached.

Although it is easy to say that asking and listening are 'always' the answer, there are clear barriers when working with families who have English as an additional language. We need to consider how we can support the parents to understand the development and learning of their child and how we can genuinely hear their views. We also have the challenge of making sure that they are clear about the full and informed implications of SEND referrals and that child protection concerns are communicated accurately and understood completely. These are difficult conversations to have at any time but when language might be a barrier and cultural expectations might differ, this is an added dilemma. Be careful not to overlook these parents because of the barriers involved. Some settings are fortunate enough to have translators on hand who can help to negotiate language barriers, but this is not always the case. Look into the support that you have within your setting and the support that is available to you through local authority services, and don't forget the myriad translation apps that are freely available if a real person isn't. Also don't forget your search can (and should) start with the expertise found in your own school community.

In many ways there are no easy answers, just as each child is unique, each parent and each family will bring with them a very personal set of characteristics. But unlike the diverse individuals that we deal with, the way forward is always very similar in nature, we need to *listen* more than we *talk*. The vast majority of parents want what's best for their children, just as we do … and if it ever appears otherwise, perhaps we need to look more carefully and listen more intently, just to be certain. There is always a way forward that occupies common ground, and our role is to facilitate finding that space of understanding, where co-construction of the child's experience between parent and practitioner can take place. Knowing where the lines are for us as practitioners and for parents can be crucial in working together. Sometimes change for both parties can be a gradual drip, drip, drip of knowledge and understanding. Trust takes time to develop, as discussed in previous chapters, and in most cases (child protection aside), however critical or emotionally loaded situations might become, or however pressing and immediate they might feel, we do have time to allow that trust to develop. We must make time to breathe deep and notice and celebrate those small steps forward in working together and understanding each other.

CONCLUSION

When thinking about difficult conversations they often go hand in hand with how we classify parents in our own minds and in our own practice. We use terms such as 'challenging parents' or those that are 'hard to reach', and whilst I realise that these terms are used in day-to-day practice, I am not sure how helpful they are long term. I have never liked the term 'hard to reach', it's a personal thing I know, but I never have, and certainly would hate to be considered in this way myself. Families can be vulnerable because we do not yet know how best to reach them, but that doesn't make *them* hard to reach. When traditional methods of engaging with families don't work and we run out of ideas it can be tempting, and completely understandable, to shift the responsibility from 'I haven't reached you yet' to 'you are hard to reach'. I get it, I really do, but I don't think it helps, particularly when the time arises that you need to prepare to talk to these 'hard-to-reach' parents about something difficult.

I think the key, if there really is one, where you struggle to communicate with certain parents, is to mentally stick with 'I haven't reached you yet, but I will', and to keep trying. If your approach isn't working, then try something different. We live in a society where there is a myriad of different ways that we can communicate, keep trying. If you feel you've messed it up with a parent in some way, don't give yourself a hard time, as we've kept saying, relationships and emotions are hard. No one has all the answers, and we all make mistakes, just show your humility and vulnerability, just keep trying. If we are able to "stay curious and generous, to stick with the messy middle of a problem" and "listen with the same passion with which we want to be heard" (Brown, 2018, p.15), then difficult conversations can and should result in outcomes that benefit all concerned. If not straight away then eventually.

Admittedly it can sometimes feel unfair to be the one that has to keep trying, sometimes having to take negative comments and accusations that are thrown our way in the process. But we really need to recognise the emotions that are discussed in Chapter 4 and not take these situations personally, no matter how personal the attack may feel at the time. Obviously, there is a limit, we do not have to stand for abusive behaviour, nor should we, but we should be the ones that remain willing and able to *lean in* and sometimes take the strain when others are unable to. Like those nursery school leaders who responded with "look, I know you are angry, but it doesn't have to be this way, let's get a coffee and sort it out". Honest, heartfelt practice sometimes means being in the middle of the messy stuff and occasionally feeling a little beaten up or beaten down (Brown, 2018, p.20). Brave practice is not always easy, and experiences, good and bad, earn us the right to give advice when tackling the hard stuff. As practitioners we need to build an environment and culture where everyone (us included) feels "safe, seen, heard, and respected" (ibid.), if we can do that, and if we are willing to connect on a very real level with parents and their children, well, then everything else, at least in theory, will just follow.

At the end of the day our conversations and our practice are always regarding that which is most precious to a parent, their child, and that is what we need to keep holding first and foremost when things get tough. As we acknowledged when we started this book, being a parent is hard, it can be exhausting, terrifying, draining, and it can be relentless. It is perfectly understandable that occasionally the result of this is a raised voice or some tears. Creating a trusting relationship with a parent who you encounter just a few minutes a day, or not at all, can be a huge challenge. But as research has proven, the potential rewards to the child (and, from our perspective, the parent) far outweigh the effort.

KEY POINTS TO TAKE AWAY FROM THIS CHAPTER

1. Sometimes, as educators, we just need to "show up and be courageous". No one has all the answers; it's about a willingness to try and work them out together.
2. Remember that parents most value personalised communication.
3. Establishing regular communication on the 'small stuff' builds a strong foundation for discussing the 'big stuff'.
4. Make sure that you are clear in your communication with parents, no jargon and acronyms, no demeaning or belittling.
5. Remember the importance of positive communication; make sure that it is not always about deficit.
6. When broaching a difficult topic be sure to allow parents to air their views first, it is important for them to feel that their viewpoint is important.
7. Ask parents and follow their lead. Stay curious, and "listen with the same passion with which we want to be heard".

TEAM ACTIVITY

Difficult Conversations

As a whole team, consider the following scenarios and the actions that you would take.

Scenario 1

Your class has not had a good day, it has been one of 'those days' where you have felt that you are constantly dealing with challenging behaviour – where it has become contagious. Your class missed ten minutes of their lunch break because they had not listened to instructions, and they still had tidying-up to do after their activity. During this time one child was particularly rude and you kept her behind to discuss her behaviour after the others were sent outside. She seemed unfazed by this, and although nothing extreme, she continued with low level provocation of the other children all afternoon. You make a note that you must discuss this with the parents when you next see them.

At the end of the day, you see this girl and her father walking back towards the classroom. The child is crying, and the father looks extremely angry. Before even reaching the classroom, he has started shouting that he has had enough of his daughter being picked on as the only black girl in the class and that it has to stop.

Scenario 2

One of the children in your pre-school room, at almost three, is really late coming out of nappies and you have been working on this with mum, who is always very happy to chat and take advice. Lately every time you change him there is bruising around his thighs and buttocks. He is quite a clumsy child who bumps and falls frequently, but you are concerned that some of the bruises look like finger imprints from the child being grabbed aggressively. What do you do?

Consider the following questions:

Are your responses consistent?
What is considered 'best practice' in these scenarios?
Is this an area that your staff would value greater guidance on?
What support is in place for you (and/or your team) in these types of situations?

REFERENCES

Brown, B. (2018). *Dare to lead: brave work, tough conversations, whole hearts.* London: Vermilion.

Chappel, J. and Ratliff, K. (2021). Factors impacting positive school–home communication: a multiple case study of family–school partnership practices in eight elementary schools in Hawai'i'. *School Community Journal*, 31(2), 9–30.

Leland, A.S. (2021). Doing family differently in school-to-home contexts: gay fathers at the schoolhouse door. *Educational Administration Quarterly*, 57(1), 143–173.

Longley, M. and Sharma, S. (2011). Listening to the voice of children and families, together. In Trodd, L. and Chivers, L. (eds), *Interprofessional working in practice: learning and working together for children and families.* Berkshire: McGraw Open University Press, 119–129.

Page, J. (2018). Characterising the principles of professional love in early childhood care and education. *International Journal of Early Years Education*, 26(2), 125–141.

Pen Green (2018). *A celebratory approach to SEND assessment in the early years.* Available from: https://www.pengreen.org/wp-content/uploads/2018/05/A-Celebratory-Approach-to-SEND-Assessment-in-Early-Years-1.pdf (accessed 14 December 2021).

Solvason, C. and Proctor, S. (2021). 'You have to find the right words to be honest': nurturing relationships between teachers and parents of children with Special Educational Needs. *Support for Learning*, 36(3), 470–485.

The National Federation of Voluntary Bodies (2007). *Informing families of their child's disability.* Available from: http://www.informingfamilies.ie/_fileupload/Informing_Families_Guidelines.pdf (accessed 10 November 2020).

Thompson, N. (2018). *Promoting equality: working with diversity and difference* (4th ed.). London: Palgrave.

Vuorine, T. (2021). 'It's in my interest to collaborate…' – parents' views of the process of interacting and building relationships with preschool practitioners in Sweden. *Early Child Development and Care*, 191(16), 2532–2544.

Whitaker, T. and Fiore, D.J. (2016). *Dealing with difficult parents* (2nd ed.). Oxon: Routledge.

CHAPTER 6

Battling Isolation and Engaging Parents at a Distance

Carla Solvason and Johanna Cliffe

If you are reading this book, it's not certain, but it's likely that you work within a supportive team. It's also likely that you see some of your colleagues socially on occasion. If not, that's probably because you already have a network of friends outside of work. (If none of this applies to you, then sorry for bringing up a sore subject, perhaps try a walking club?) This chapter is not a long one, and even though the chapter title might suggest it, we are not suggesting that you set up some type of school Tinder, or home help. In the last five chapters we have talked at length about how important it is that parents feel that their views are *listened to*, that they feel understood and valued, but our own research suggests that over recent years many parents feel increasingly isolated. We'll look at some of the reasons for that isolation shortly, but what Covid has proven to us all is that isolation can impact extremely negatively upon mental health. During the pandemic, for every person we knew who was battling the virus, we knew another who was battling anxiety and depression.

Very few of you reading this book will be trained psychologists, therapists, or counsellors, and that is not where this chapter is going. Throughout this book we have highlighted the needs of parents, as opposed to the needs of the school. We have stressed that anything that impacts positively on parents and families will also impact positively upon the child. That even though supporting parents seems tangential to the serious job of education, happy parents equal happy children and happy children are more ready to learn. Think of any steps taken to support parents as treating the root cause of a problem, rather than the symptoms. We promise you; the effort will be worthwhile.

REFLECTION POINT

When, as a setting, you consider 'the adverse life experiences' of children, is parent mental health in there? Remember the toll that experiences such as divorce, illness, unemployment, and bereavement can have on the adults involved, as well as the children.

SOME CAUSES OF ISOLATION

A Reduction in Local Family Services

In conversations with Maintained Nursery School (MNS) leaders, several of them mentioned the significant increase that they were seeing in parent mental health issues. This was around two years *before* the onset of Covid and the additional isolation that the lockdowns caused. One leader put this deterioration down to the decline in support services for children. She explained that the termination of services such as health visiting and post-natal support groups, not only impacted upon the parents, but also upon their interaction with their children, meaning that the effect was seen across two generations. She explained:

> We've got an awful lot more moms with more significant mental health issues. It's not just postnatal depression, it's quite severe postnatal depression that no one's picked up … We are getting the children showing the symptoms, but you sometimes think, the actual history of that is because of the attachment disorder, early neglect and things like that …
>
> (Solvason, Webb, and Sutton-Tsang, 2020, p.50)

Another leader explained how many of the opportunities for parents to socialise that were previously provided by the local authority, such as parents' and toddlers' groups and baby ballet had now stopped, and that health visitors were no longer running informative workshops, such as baby massage, or weaning. This resulted, the leader explained, in some parents becoming "very socially isolated" (ibid., p.45). It also resulted in many of the MNS staff themselves trying to find ways to fill some of the gaps left behind, for example, supporting families in accessing housing, or taking them to food banks.

Now let's be clear we are not for one minute suggesting that the end of a long teaching day you all fill your car with parents and drive them to the food bank, no, absolutely no. (Those practitioners who were doing similar were running themselves into the ground – it absolutely is *not* sustainable.) But what we would like is for you to be aware that many of the parent support groups that parents (or you) had access to some years ago, no longer exist. On top of which, we know that more traditional family structures, where support might have been given by grandparents, aunts, or uncles, are also increasingly fragmented, particularly with increased social mobility. As a result, many inexperienced parents are left to flounder, and are in desperate need of advice and reassurance.

Dealing with Children with Extreme Needs

As Carla said in the introductory chapter, being a parent can be all-consuming, you never get to clock off; but dealing with a child with extreme needs can bring far more extreme challenges. In their research Sedibe and Fourie (2018) found that parents of children with SEN could often blame themselves for their child's diagnosis and feel deep shame as a result. This could result in those parents choosing to isolate themselves and cutting off social contact. Parents can also find social expeditions, and the reactions of those that do not understand their child's behaviour, just too difficult to manage, resulting in fewer and fewer outings into the outside world. It can be very difficult to 'fit'.

> This has been my sister's experience with her own daughter. My niece is now 18 and still struggles with extreme anxiety. The anxiety has meant that she was unable to cope in the school system and after a number of years of battling my sister gave up trying. My niece still cannot cope with the demands of life without my sister by her side to support her. As a result, my sister's own separate, social life stopped 18 years ago.
>
> *Carla*

There can also be a sense of grieving when you are raising a child with SEND. Hess et al. (2006, p.148) explain this as the loss of that child for whom the parents had such high hopes. Finally, Orphan (2004, p.112) describes the exhaustion that resulted from her coping with her son's extreme needs and watching her husband leaving for work "having not had enough sleep and struggling to function, but it's still easier than being home".

The very specific struggles of a parent of a child with SEND can mean that the likelihood of finding someone who understands your struggles reduces dramatically, and this is where settings can help. They can do this by providing opportunities to bring parents together, by creating occasions for those parents who *would* value it, to take part in activities with children and other families. This could be stay and play, a regular coffee/open evening, workshops, or a game of rounders in the summer. These occasions will, no doubt, be trial and error as you explore your families' varied needs in terms of timings and forms of contact (and, equally, respecting the choice of those who choose to *not* interact) but they could potentially provide opportunities for understanding and supportive friendships to emerge amongst parents. One SEND teacher explained why friendships between parents could be so valuable. They said:

> [I've] got two parents that I'm working with at the moment, and they have known each other now, been coming to sessions now, for six or seven weeks, and they have just this week

exchanged telephone numbers which is so exciting! But it's really nice, because at last, you know, they feel comfortable enough to do that social thing! ... They've just worked out their children are very similar, and actually they could go together, places, and share that horrible feeling my child is the one that's causing all the problems instead of being on their own and doing it. And I think that's ... huge! And really nice actually that they find somebody to do that with... And they could be slightly less stressed ... and that will ... not pass that on to the children ... And just have somebody, that understands when they're having a bad day, what that actually means.

As stronger links are made between parents in your settings, the sources of support available to them will increase exponentially. And the firmer a safety net will be in place for the children of those families. Yet, we are aware that there have been fewer opportunities than ever to bring parents together in this way over the last few years, and we explore some of the implications of that below.

PARTNERSHIP LESSONS THAT WE CAN LEARN FROM COVID

We discussed whether we should include a chapter about Covid in this book. As it is such an emotive topic, there are many competing voices in the literature at the point of writing, and we were not sure if this book was the place to add more. We didn't want to just reframe much of what is already being said or fall into the trap of merely voicing empty platitudes. Whilst fairly confident that we can all agree Covid and the subsequent lockdowns have been a huge presence in all our lives, it has left many of us now, all these months on, in between wanting to *tune in* and *tune out* of yet more discussions around the pandemic. For many of you, and for us too, work–life balance has become a distant blur and we may, quite possibly, have all worked harder over the last two years than ever before, under fluidly insecure and unprecedented conditions.

Yet, there are also some seeds of hope for positive change. Hansen and Cillo (2020, p.5) described lockdown as the "opportunity to observe stillness, analyse reality as it is and it was, and question the possibilities for this uncertain future". Roy (2020), cited in Cameron and Moss (2020, p.16), claims that the pandemic and the *new* ways of working and being provide a "gateway between one world and the next" and that it is a personal as well as societal decision to consider whether we are ready to imagine another world. Presumably this new world involves *a lot* of computer screens. So, as we move further into living within this *new normal,* whatever normal was and now is, what would it be useful to take with us and what should we leave firmly behind?

As we reflect on our own experiences as well as those of family and friends working in different educational contexts throughout lockdown, I'm sure that we can all agree that the expectation to create and maintain some kind of routine, something that felt familiar and yet was so fundamentally and completely alien, was a challenge to us all. And then experiences of *life* during the pandemic were so diverse. Positive for some families, with increased family time and opportunities to reconnect, as they managed to navigate competing priorities. But for other families the many lockdowns brought huge challenges, on all levels and often totally beyond their control. You do not need me to tell you the juggling that we all did and are still doing to maintain our own equilibrium and navigate our own ways through, I know you will all have your own stories, your own highs, and your lows.

There is an old African proverb which says, 'it takes a village to raise a child' and I think it is fair to say that during lockdown communities, parents, and educators, came together to work together differently to empower families, safeguard children, and continue to *educate* in the best way possible (May and Coulston, 2021, p.104). It felt like a moment when the phrases we utter rather flippantly such as "we are all in this together" had far greater meaning. Let's be honest, our government has not been the most shining example when it comes to equity of experience, but as parents, educators, and children, it really did feel that we were, and still are, in this together. So, what can we take forward from these experiences together to reimagine a better partnership moving forward into a better world?

REFLECTION POINT

Take a minute to consider your own experience of lockdown and working *with* your families. If you had to sum up the main learning points that you could take away from your experiences, positive and negative, what would they be? Why?

APPRECIATION ACROSS THE DIVIDE

Although reporting from New Zealand, May and Coulston (2021) made the argument that in the coming together during lockdown the parent–educator relationships became stronger. They commented that communication and dialogue with those families that they previously *had yet to reach* was, in particular, more evident, and therefore partnerships more evenly spread throughout all the families in their communities. Increased mutual trust and respect developed, and was nurtured, within shared difficulty and lockdown experiences. In the UK this is sometimes referred to more colloquially as "the Blitz spirit", a phrase taken from wartime, referring to the notion that when facing something dangerous and overwhelmingly lifechanging it is within our human nature to pull together, to offer the hand of help and friendship to family, friend, or stranger alike. There is no space within this relationship for an *us and them* divide, so differences become invisible, and we are left with a sense of belonging and community as being key to survival.

In our own experience with higher education students the continued challenges were thick and fast. For those working from home, navigating studying around their own children, fitting their lectures around their children's home education, balancing those emotional moments when their own children were struggling, and then pasting on a smile in their own paid employment, was gruelling for many. Anxiety and exhaustion were palpable throughout this time. And the only thing left that we could offer was understanding. Understanding that despite all efforts, there was no hope of maintaining any sort of stability during this time. We were all firefighting, all just doing our best, and it was perfectly acceptable when work was late, and meetings were cancelled. (Johanna and her colleague likened it to playing in a real-life game of Whack-a-Mole, who knew what was coming next.) A lot was just about treading water to stay afloat, and more pressure was not going to help anything, not then, and not now. But within these moments trusting bonds of humanity were nurtured as we all tried to just make it through together.

Shortly after lockdown ended and we were released back into the wild, a colleague and I ran an Early Years Network meeting. The idea of these meetings is that Early Years leaders (reception teachers, nursery managers, and so on) come together and explore an area of practice development. The topic for this particular session was *meant* to be social capital ... we only reached the first slide. As an 'opener' we asked the attendees to chat with one another about the highs and lows of their term so far and what they saw as a challenge. They didn't stop talking for the next two hours. They found it hugely cathartic sharing with like-minded others who *understood* what they saw as the impact of Covid and the ways that they were struggling in settings with huge gaps in the children's development and continual staff shortages. Now this may sound a little depressing, but anyone within the vicinity of that meeting would not have thought so, as the session was peppered throughout with raucous laughter. The chance to 'offload', to 'let off steam' was the perfect antidote for the relentlessly depressing situations that all of the practitioners had been enduring. All of us left that get together with our spirits lifted. And this very human contact is something that we cannot replicate via a meeting on a screen. At heart we are social animals, and let's remember that looking forward.

Carla

As parents were faced with the challenge of teaching as well as parenting, some came to more fully understand the challenges of the educator's role, resulting in a renewed respect and empathy for our profession. Other parents relished the challenges of this new responsibility and saw the potential for a career change, or, even to home-school on a more permanent basis. There was a shift in the concept that we, as educators, solely and effortlessly spewed out fonts of resources and ideas, to the idea that exciting opportunities could be created when teachers and parents worked together in truly collaborative ways. And within this collaboration concepts of 'difference' between parents, as mentioned above, became null and void. The type of work a parent did made no difference, whether or not they changed out of their pyjamas made no difference, as Sylva et al. (2004, p.1) stated "what parents do is more important than who parents are". May and Coulston (2021, p.103) discussed parents making dolls' houses out of cardboard and sharing pictures for other parents to try it, too, taking walks in local areas and photographing wonders in nature that would previously have gone unnoticed, and enjoying the fun of pavement drawings, as examples of contributions that made up a "spiral of families and children contributing". Their research further evidenced the positive impacts of parents' growing confidence in what they *could* do, and educators were seen to engage more purposefully with parents' efforts to support their children (ibid.). During this time some educators were able to move past the tokenistic acknowledgement of parents' views before getting on with the serious business of teaching, to a place where parents' ideas were truly listened to, valued, and built upon. During distance learning, education became an authentically shared endeavour filled with agency, innovation, and creativity by all of those involved.

So, the question this raises, is what if this could continue? What would be possible then?

REFLECTION POINT

Think about your own setting and the provision offered during lockdown:

- Did lockdown provide you an opportunity for shared educative experiences with parents that were new to your practice?
- If yes, were these experiences positive? Why?
- Were they challenging? Why?

- How much of this have you held on to as life has "gone back to normal"? (If any.)
- Have you witnessed any change in the way you and the parents of the children that you care for view each other?
- What does this look and feel like?

TECHNOLOGY

Many of you will have your own tales of using educational technology to stay connected during the lockdowns, be it good old-fashioned telephone, Teams, Zoom, Skype, or many of the other options available. And we probably all have endless stories regarding small children, cats, dogs, and other pets muscling in on the action. (Our own and others.) It's strange to think that a type of communication that seemed otherworldly and terrifying to many of us just a couple of years ago is now the norm.

However, although online conferencing supported educational provision in general, the remit of this book is to consider partnership, so how did it support that? We all know that using technology to support parent partnership is not a new phenomenon, many of us do it every day if you consider phone calls, text messages, and emails. There are also all the extra options for recording and sharing assessment, Tapestry or Dojo for example. The official line on the use of technology with parents comes from Ofsted's (2011, p.9) report where they clearly state that where partnership works *well* technology *complements* traditional communication methods (and its use is particularly advocated for working parents and those parents who cannot easily 'get in' just to schools). Whilst these methods were not designed, originally, to *replace* traditional dialogues and face-to-face communication with parents, when the pandemic hit, they became the mainstay of any dialogue with parents, along with a whole host of other virtual options being thrown in, to boot. But what now? Whilst face-to-face and human connection should never be marginalised or taken for granted, we have learnt a range of ways of communicating with those who cannot make it into settings, and it is worth taking at least some of this forward.

Wilson and Waddel (2020, p.10) reported that from an early help and multi-agency perspective, there were mixed reviews regarding digital practices in England. In some authorities, the ability to offer virtual support packages, meant that whilst help for some was diminished, other families received help and support quicker than they would have done previously. One children's centre coordinator commented that they were considering retaining a significant level of digital support as this was seen as positive for parents with anxiety and other mental health challenges (ibid., p.11). Not only were parents who were previously marginalised by the demands of face-to-face meetings more included and empowered, online meetings also enabled professionals from many different disciplines to get together more easily than diaries and geography would formerly have allowed. So there are, undoubtedly, some practices that are worth taking forward. Online meetings could replace the awful parents' evening carousel, for example.

Obviously, it would be remiss of us not to note the shadow side of technology and the pandemic, regarding the digital divide that emerged between families of different socio-economic backgrounds. And yes, there has to be more support and more awareness of what support can be put into place to support *all* families, including those for whom purchasing expensive technological equipment is going to be more difficult. But as we are writing this for a parent *not* to own a mobile device would be rare. Moving forward it is definitely worth us embracing virtual spaces as an alternative way to connect with those parents and families who struggle to be present within the educational environment.

REFLECTION POINT

Can you think of some parents and families that you actually had more contact with during the pandemic? How might technology be used to sustain that increased involvement?

A FINAL THOUGHT ABOUT PARENTS' SELF-EFFICACY AND SELF-ESTEEM

An international research project by Atiles et al. (2021, p.73) noted challenges that parents faced in navigating their new educator role during lockdown learning. These challenges included a lack of confidence with technology as well as challenges with literacy and other academic skills. Whilst this study was not conducted in the UK there will undoubtedly be parallels with family skillsets within the UK. This disconnect can have damaging impacts upon parents' self-esteem even when it is unintended. Here we return to the content of the first chapters of this book, where we tend to treat all parents as the same and have the same expectations of all parents. How we want parents to support their child's learning is usually predefined and pre-coded. So how can we be more open to ways of engaging parents who don't have some of these fundamental skills? He can we engage parents in alternative ways?

It is perfectly reasonable that some parents will not want to admit to the academic difficulties they might have, I mean, who does like to air their vulnerabilities? And even if parents are comfortable admitting that they are not able to read, or that they are not good with numbers, how can we best support this? We cannot send all parents who fail to meet the literacy and numeracy levels of attainment that we would like them to have off to adult learning programmes. Some parents will simply not have the capability in these areas. For most it will not be that they *didn't bother* studying, but they simply *couldn't* and still *can't*. And if you think about it, again, we are simply viewing this from the position of parents being more *useful* to us, in their children reaching *our* intended outcomes.

> In my own teaching practice, I worked with a range of parents who had very different literacy levels and learning needs, as well as with parents for whom English was not their first language. Although I did always try to be sensitive in my dealings with the families that I worked with, I now look back and ask was there more that I could have done?
>
> *Johanna*

REFLECTION POINT

A simple activity to encourage practitioners to consider other methods of supporting communication is to hand them a menu written in Greek. Now, whereas most of us may be vaguely familiar with French, German, Italian, or even Spanish, enough so that we might be able to make an educated guess, languages such as Greek, or Hungarian, with their own alphabet, can be totally and utterly impenetrable. (Of course, there's always one smart aleck who is multi-lingual, but generally people are left befuddled.) Then hand them the same menu, with very small and simple illustrations next to each item. A bowl of soup, a fish, a roast chicken leg. Now, we still may not be sure what, precisely, the dishes are, but at least we could make a far more informed choice. Remember, there is a whole range of ways to communicate, consider them all when you are struggling to understand or to make yourself understood.

In Atiles et al.'s (2021) study, pictures were used to support parents in decoding instructions and for examples of what they needed to do online if the technology was new to them. We often see 'screenshots' in sets of instructions for accessing systems and resources online. Why not implement this notion of using images more across all of our interactions with parents if we know that it will help some with access? The same study used the example of a parent who was unable to read being encouraged to recognise the knowledge that he *did* have and encouraged to draw on oral storytelling to support his child's developing cognition. And other parents were discretely and subtly coached at the same time as their children, which worked as the best way forward for all parties. While vastly different, these strategies all had in common one central feature, to *include* and *encourage* all parents in ways that were unique to and suited their requirements. We are used to employing a range of approaches to differentiate for children's needs, let's start to be more aware of parents' needs in the same way.

How we support those parents who might require alternative forms of communication needs some careful thinking. When we do provide extra measures for parents we need to be mindful that these increased efforts are not noticed by others, as this could negatively impact on parents' self-confidence and self-efficacy. Our advice would be that the same, more easily accessed, forms of communication are used across the board, for all parents. Those parents who need the prompts will be supported (including those who may not have disclosed that they need additional support), and those parents who are perfectly literate will read the information and ignore the extra prompts. Like the menu. Instead of sending out a text message send out a voice message. Simple. The pandemic forced many of us into positions where we needed to reconsider how we communicate with parents, and that is not entirely a bad thing. Moving forward, it would seem, it remains up to each of us, as individuals and as settings, to decide on which new strategies, developed during lockdown, we keep. To decide which new ways of working were so successful that we take them forward into our new normal practice, whatever that ends up being.

CONCLUSION

The final point in this chapter is rather short; however, it is probably the most important. Lockdown saw us taking chances, taking risks, trying out things to make possible what at first appeared impossible. For example, around the country in the UK, transition materials were videoed and posted on accessible social media so that parents and children could feel more at ease with starting new provisions or seeing the face of and hearing the voice of their new teacher. Pascal and Bertram (2021, p.28) discussed how garden visits and similar were included in those settling-in periods where parents would previously have been welcomed into the setting. These were all small and relatively easy changes to make possible what seemed to have become impossible. Bucket loads of initiative and creativity emerged as practitioners and settings faced barriers to their pre-existing ways of doing things. Moving forward, how might we continue to do this? How can we retain those lessons learnt, having lived, thought these experiences, and gained the skills that we have developed in 'changing things up' and thinking outside the box? How creative can we be in our expectations of and our interactions with parents?

KEY POINTS TO TAKE AWAY FROM THIS CHAPTER

1. Be aware that many parents feel very isolated within their community and that this can impact upon mental wellbeing.
2. Equally, be aware that coping with a child with extreme SEND can be even more isolating – and involve even more extreme emotions.
3. Recognise the impact that Covid has had upon the mental health of many.
4. Embrace the many forms of communication that Covid enabled – and hold on to those that are useful. Likewise, be aware of the gaps where parents may struggle with communication and consider alternative approaches. For example, voicemails instead of written text.
5. Consider the range of practices that were implemented to involve parents during Covid, and those that it will be worth taking forward.

TEAM ACTIVITY

As a whole setting collate examples of successful, innovative, and creative practices for involving parents that were developed during lockdown.

Why did these approaches work?
How do you know that these approaches were valued by parents?
Which of these approaches are worth taking forward as a whole team?

REFERENCES

Atiles, J.T., Almodóvar, M., Chavarría Vargas, A., Dias, M.J.A. and León, I.M.Z. (2021). International responses to COVID-19: challenges faced by early childhood professionals. *European Early Childhood Education Research Journal*, 29(1), 66–78.

Cameron, C. and Moss, P. (2020). *Transforming early childhood in England.* London: UCL Press.

Hansen, C.S. and Cillo, M.N. (2020). *Breaking reality: a rhizoanalysis of insurrectionary politics in the 21st century.* Available at: file:///C:/Users/TLI/Downloads/PROJECTPP.pdf (Accessed: 20 January 2022).

Hess, R. S., Molina, A. M. and Kozleski, E. B. (2006) Until somebody hears me: parent voice and advocacy in special educational decision making. *British Journal of Special Education*, 33(3) 148–157. https://doi.org/10.1111/j.1467-8578.2006.00430.x

May, H. and Coulston, A. (2021). He Whānau Manaaki kindergartens, Aotearoa New Zealand: a pandemic outreach in new political times. *European Early Childhood Education Research Journal*, 29(1), 96–108.

Ofsted (2011). *Schools and parents.* Available from: https://assets.publishing.service.gov.uk/government/uploads/system/uploads/attachment_data/file/413695/Schools_and_parents.doc (accessed 20 January 2022).

Orphan, A. (2004). *Moving on: supporting parents of children with SEN.* London: Fulton.

Pascal, C. and Bertram, T. (2021). What do young children have to say? Recognising their voices, wisdom, agency and need for companionship during the COVID pandemic. *European Early Childhood Education Research Journal*, 29(1), 21–34.

Sedibe, M. and Fourie, J. (2018). Exploring opportunities and challenges in parent–school partnerships in special needs schools in the Gauteng Province, South Africa. *Interchange*, 49(4), 433–444. https://doi.org/10.1007/s10780-018-9334-5.

Solvason, C., Webb, R. and Sutton-Tsang, S. (2020). What is left...?: the implications of losing maintained nursery schools for vulnerable children and families in England. *Children and Society*. https://authorservices.wiley.com/api/pdf/fullArticle/16752045.

Sylva et al. (2004). The Effective Provision of Pre-School Education (EPPE) project: Findings from pre-school to end of key stage 1. Available from: https://dera.ioe.ac.uk/18189/2/SSU-SF-2004-01.pdf (accessed 20 January 2022).

Wilson, H. and Waddell, S. (2020). *Covid-19 and early intervention understanding the impact, preparing for recovery.* Available from: https://www.eif.org.uk/report/covid-19-and-early-intervention-understanding-the-impact-preparing-for-recovery (accessed 20 January 2022).

Conclusion

Carla Solvason

If you have managed to read all of this book, then we are delighted that you have undertaken the journey with us. We hope, at the very least that some of the views and ideas presented might have caused you to stop and question your practices. We hope at best that it might have given you some clear ideas for change. We also hope that you've been able to discuss some of the ideas that we suggest with others; and if you've managed to review your values and practices as a whole school, well, there's no more that we can ask. Our work here is done. We've aced it. (And you too, obvs.)

In this conclusion I am going to review the key points that we have visited as a recap and to remind you of some targets for your future travels.

> 1. Let's be more aware that at times the demands that we put on parents as educators can simply be too much.

First, I reminded you how hard being a parent can be through sharing my own, often painful, experience. I must admit, if you had all stopped reading after the introduction then this book would still have been worthwhile in my eyes. This was (unashamedly) my key objective – for those practitionerswho are unaware, or may have forgotten, to recognise and appreciate the sometimes relentless toil of parenting.

DOI: 10.4324/9781003191209-7

> 2. Remember that no two parents are the same, so it is important that we stop treating them as though they are.

What is also extremely important to remember is that all parents are different, they are not one single species that thinks and behaves in a regulated way. They are not a shoal of fish, or a murmuration of birds, or any other metaphor that involves animals that look identical acting in an identical way. From your Earth Mothers to those that shout "dive, dive, dive" to usher their children out of the car whilst parked on the no parking zone outside of the school gates (come on, I wasn't the only one, was I?). From parents who lunch to parents fitting in demanding jobs around single parenthood, and perhaps an elderly ill parent to boot. For every parent who demands more homework another will think it a total waste of time and a huge pain in the behind. Although one parent may relish time spent in their child's school, whether dressing children for nativity or hearing them read, another will dread it. Whilst one parent will prioritise their child attaining good grades, another will prioritise their sporting success, or their creativity or simply their happiness, whatever the source of that may be. Whilst one parent will take pleasure in preparing super-healthy snacks for a movie, another will see it as a great opportunity for the family to indulge in chocolates and popcorn. Each and every parent is different, with their own values and their own aims for their child.

> 3. So how do we embrace the vast diversity of ideas, values, and skills (okay, yes, and challenges) that a diverse range of parents bring to our settings?

How do we find out what type of people those parents that we are starting a new year with are? Well, it may be stating the obvious, but we get to know them, we listen to them. The brutal truth is that we become so used, as educationalists and carers, to giving instructions, to making demands, that we can forget to make the space to listen to alternative viewpoints, to new perspectives and suggestions. We can become so *busy* that we lose that key skill of all practitioners, the ability to reflect. How can we genuinely listen to parents and how can we show that we are listening? Not just to those confident and educated parents on the Parent Teacher Association, but to the busy working parents, the parents struggling with difficult domestic situations, the parents battling mental health issues, the parents with English as a second language, the parents with learning difficulties, the parents in poverty. What are we doing about these others? How are *we* tackling the communication issue, rather than just labelling *them* hard to reach?

---

4. What do we really want from the parents of the children who we work with? Partners fully invested in their children's education, or, effectively, unpaid teaching assistants to do our bidding? And how can we create a parent partnership that is most suited to their values, their aspirations, to their lives?

Something that we are also guilty of as practitioners, and something which can cause a barrier between educator and parent, is making assumptions. Of narrowing our views to focus solely on our own, or our setting's agenda. Often our aim is to achieve the targets that we have set (or that have been imposed upon us) and we can struggle to see beyond those. As settings we can (consciously or subconsciously) formulate preconceived ideas about what the good parent 'looks like' and how they behave, and we can view anyone who does not fit that mould as coming up short. A child submits a shoddy attempt at a homework project, that parent is disinterested, a child has incomplete cooking ingredients, that parent is lazy. Heaven forbid that there are events going on outside of the setting that the parent may need to prioritise over a 1920s schoolboy outfit for the school trip. Divorce, care responsibilities, long working hours, domestic abuse, mental illness, poverty … none of these, it would seem, not even death, serve as valid excuses for not writing in that blasted reading record. How can we enable parents to support their child's educational journey in a way that fits in with their life rather than simply making demands of them?

> 5. Think about your own setting, your staff, your children, your own families. Are they a kaleidoscope of colour that reflects your community or are they shades of grey?

As settings, how can we be more open to not just *accepting* but to welcoming and embracing difference? How can we see diversity, in appearance, values, and ideas, as something to be enjoyed, something to be celebrated, rather than fearing it? To see varieties in colour, nationality, sexuality, appearance, language, culture, and so on as rich sources to be harvested. To see them as learning opportunities for us, as educators, as well as the children. I was dumbstruck when one of our students, just last year, was sent home from her *voluntary* placement for having pink hair. I had pink hair (or it may have been lilac) at the time. What difference did that make to who she was, to who I was? How does hair colour impact upon our ability to educate, our ability to care? It doesn't. Acts like these, demanding conformity, are not about care and education, they are about control. Regulatory bleach blonde is acceptable, other colours are not. They are about fearing 'difference' and finding comfort in 'same'. What messages does your setting convey about such things?

One nursery leader I spoke with talked about SEND as an opportunity rather than a chore. She saw the benefits of taking on children with extreme needs as two-fold. First, that having a range of diversity in the setting clearly reflected the community outside of the setting walls; and second, and this is what I would like you to really take on board here, she saw it as an opportunity for them, as a staff, to learn. I particularly remember our discussion about a child who was deaf and blind. The leader discussed how they, as educationalists, learned about the importance of smell (his teaching assistant made sure to always wear the same perfume to work) and touch in their communications with him. Her attitude was not one of *"boy, he was a challenge to our resources"* but *"we learned so much from him"*. Are you a setting that sees the challenge of difference as an opportunity to grow?

6. There has to be a trusting human connection between parent and educationalist, whereby you understand and respect one another's knowledge and experience in light of your own limitations.

As a setting, are there strong bonds of trust between you as a staff? If there are not, then you may struggle to create trusting partnerships with parents, so that may be a good place to start. And I don't mean those awful staff development days where you go rock climbing together before falling back on one another or sit on each other's knees in a circle (cringe!), I mean just being open with one another, sharing strengths, weaknesses, and fears. Looking to one another for guidance, for support. I have been fortunate enough to work with a team, for a long time now, that thrives on openness, on humility, and on respect for one another's skills alongside an acceptance of weaknesses. I mean the sort of team that when someone new makes a mistake (and thinks that they are going to be sacked) we are all happy to comfort said new person with our stories of the monumental cockups that we've made. We are human and perfectly imperfect. And this, for me, is just how a team should be (although I'm open to hearing that there's an even better type of team out there). This also means that when I worked with someone from another team, and she shared her wisdom with me of 'never admit your mistakes', she immediately lost my trust. If you don't take the blame yourself, then who is taking it for you?

In the chapter on trust, we discussed how it is intrinsically linked with vulnerability. With those who you trust, you are able to share your disasters as well as your triumphs. To look for guidance as well as praise. How do you create trusting relationships with parents within your setting whilst retaining professionalism? How do you create a culture which says, 'we both want what is best for your child – we are in this together'? It has to start with you not pretending to have all of the answers but looking to one another for advice and guidance, with you valuing what the parent has to say as the person who knows that child best, the expert in the child's life.

> 7. Regardless of whether it is found in policy or not, emotion is central to education and care.

I'll not repeat what has been said in Chapter 3, but it is a sad fact that in the privatisation and marketisation of education and care the human aspect has been lost. Educators are no longer autonomous, fellow explorers alongside the children in their care, individuals who can make an impromptu trip to the canal with their brood to see the frog spawn that has appeared overnight. No, oh no, what of phonics, what of the assessment on 3-D shapes? Practitioners are now units of production who must learn how to best manipulate objectives, materials, children, and parents to produce the best assessment results possible. They are merely a cog in the machinery of education.

But despite the policy culture in the UK, education is still dependent upon relationships, and educators (and parents) are still people. A long time ago I did some research into the impact of a high school becoming a specialist sports college. I was concerned that those children who were rubbish at sport would be made to feel more of a failure because of the school's shift in focus. I was wrong, the children were barely aware of the specialism of the school. There was just one thing that was key to the children in terms of their overall enjoyment of school and their engagement with certain subjects, that was whether they felt that the person teaching them *liked* them. It came up again and again in their responses. What was key for these children was that the teachers really *knew* them, that they saw them as the individual that they were. And it was on exactly the same basis that, as a mother, I made my assessment of my own children's settings. Key for me was whether I felt that the staff *liked* my child, whether it seems that they *cared* enough to get to know them, to get to know me.

If we accept that, at its heart, education is about people and relationships, and that people are a whole tangle of emotions, the thought of trying to *eliminate* those emotions from the education process becomes a little ridiculous. They are always going to be there. So, then the question becomes how we should acknowledge them. How we should make space for them and feel more confident in managing them. It is important that we are clear about the relationship between emotions and professionalism in our working lives, and that we feel confident in our understanding of that. I need not go into the impact that the suppressing of emotions can have over time. As a nation our statistics concerning depression and other mental health issues say it all. So, as a setting, what are some ways that you can support one another's emotional wellbeing (and I include parents in this) and be more aware of, and more open about, your own?

> 8. Difficult conversations with parents are always going to happen, how can you enable them to happen as painlessly as is possible?

This is very much tied to the point above, in that difficult conversations cannot happen without emotions being involved. There is going to be embarrassment, hurt, anger, feelings of incompetency, of failure. As Johanna advises in her chapter which tackles emotions (Chapter 4), we should 'lean into' these feelings, rather than pretend that they don't exist to make ourselves feel better. What is important is that we validate the emotions that might result from this difficult conversation. Like the teachers in the SEND school who allowed parents to rant without judgement, aware of the awful time that they had been through. Like the nursery leaders who said that they understood why the parent was angry, and perhaps they could get a cup of tea and talk it through. Several times during this book we have made mention of the intensity of emotions that you can feel as a parent who wants to protect their child.

Most, if not all, parents will have felt a totally irrational amount of rage or upset at some point in relation to their child. The parents of the children who you work with will feel this, too, especially if you are telling them something about their child that they do not want to hear. When this happens, stand beside them to show that you understand. Listen to them, let them know that they are not alone, but that this can be worked out *together*.

---

9. In a world that has become more isolated than ever, aim to bring people together.

When I spoke with nursery school leaders a few years ago they told me that mental health issues were becoming a 'huge' issue. They put this down to the withdrawal of many local, social services because of funding cuts. So, no more mums and toddlers, no more baby ballet. And the result of this was extreme isolation for many of the parents. Fast forward to today and that isolation, as a result of Covid, is more extreme than it has ever been. But all of us need time with people that 'get us', people who understand the things that we are dealing with; and as a new mum, or first-time mum especially, you need lots of reassurance. How does that happen when you don't have the chance to socialise with anyone in a similar position?

The teachers in the SEND school discussed how much more extreme the isolation could be as a parent of a child with extreme needs. For example, how painful the experience of taking the child out to a public place could be, a place where no one understood your child, or the behaviours that they were demonstrating. The isolation, and the daily demands of dealing with a child with extreme needs, can have significant impacts upon a parent's mental health. The poor mental health of a parent will impact upon the wellbeing of the child. The result of this will be that the child is in an insecure place and is in no position to learn. Remember, whatever creates a more secure environment for the child will impact positively on the child's development. So, if you need a clear reason to even contemplate the social life of the parents of your children, remember *happy parents equals happy children*. Happy children have a far greater chance of educational success than their anxious peers.

Therefore, as I hope is clear from our final chapter, we are not for one minute suggesting that you become drinking buddies with the average parents and yoga partners with the teetotal Earth Mothers … good heavens no! What we are suggesting, instead, is that you find opportunities to bring parents together in the hope that friendships might develop between them. Whether that is open mornings at the setting or events held elsewhere, for those parents who are not experiencing the social interaction provided by paid employment, these opportunities to socialise with peers might be invaluable.

During the pandemic we have all discovered innovative new ways of communicating with one another. It is highly likely that, as a setting, this has included alternative means of interacting with parents. What effective practices can you take forward? How can we squeeze some good, some positives, out of what has been, essentially, an extremely dark period?

And that, folks, is all that we have. As I said at the start of this book, if you are already doing all of these things, then keep doing them. You are fabulous and should feel extremely smug at this point. If the culture of your school is poles apart from the ideas presented here, well why not start with some very small steps? It may be that you are making these steps alone, be brave and lead by example. If you can get your colleagues on board, well that is fantastic; and hopefully you can use some of the activities included in this book to think about some genuine, setting-wide changes.

Index

Lightning Source UK Ltd.
Milton Keynes UK
UKHW020436090922
408582UK00005B/39